Contents

Helping Your Schoolchild

by

Carol Baker

Longman

Longman Group UK Limited
Longman House
Burnt Hill, Harlow, Essex CM20 2JE, England
and Association Companies throughout the World

First published 1991

British Library Cataloguing in Publication Data
Baker, Carol 1944 –
   Help your schoolchild. – (Successful parenting guides).
   1. Great Britain. Education. Role of parents
   I. Title   II. Series
   370

   ISBN 0-582-05033-2

Set in 10/11 Gill Sans

Produced by Longman Group (FE) Ltd.

Printed in Hong Kong

Where you fit in: the importance of parental support

Introduction

Starting school is a significant step in the life of every child – and their parents. For eleven years or more our children will spend a large part of their days away from us in the care of people we may hardly know. There are areas of our children's life we can know little about directly. We must rely on our children's subjective version of events and upon information we may be able to glean from teachers. Everything that happens at school happens at one remove from us. We can no longer be by our children's side to remind, to prompt, to encourage, to commiserate or to point out how they might do things better. Our children will achieve their own successes and make their own mistakes and we will not be directly involved. They are growing up and becoming independent.

However, as parents we still have a vital role in our children's education. Research shows that when parents have a positive attitude towards education and can support learning at home then educational achievements are significantly improved. But we don't just help educationally. At some point we have to deal with emotional problems: our child may be reluctant to go to school, find it hard to make friends, or fail to get on with their teacher. Helping our child emotionally and socially is every bit as important as helping with school work. Unhappy children are educationally disadvantaged. They are too distracted to concentrate on learning.

Home and school have a direct impact upon each other. If our child is unhappy at school we will experience the backlash at home – he may be tense, touchy, withdrawn or even aggressive. Similarly, if there are problems at home – perhaps because of marital difficulties, illness, or a new baby in the family – this can affect a child's work or behaviour at school. The closer the relationship between home and school, the more effectively each can understand and support the child.

Good communication between home and school helps advance a child's educational performance. If schools keep parents well informed about their educational aims and methods, encouraging them to ask questions and become involved, then parents can provide practical help and encouragement for their children.

Why parents hold back
No one would pretend it's always easy to know how best to help our children when they have problems at school. We can feel disadvantaged for any of the following reasons.

- We find it difficult to establish a reliable picture of what's happening because information reaches us through our children who inevitably have a subjective picture of the situation.

- Negative feelings about our own school

days may come back to haunt us the minute we step over the school threshold.

- We are not directly involved in the situation and therefore we cannot intervene directly.

- We may lack practical know-how either about how schools work or about how to help our child with some particular academic problem.

- We may worry about how the school sees us. Will we be labelled neurotic or fussy?

However helpless we may sometimes feel, there is invariably something we can do. We can often help our child by just talking a problem through with them, providing moral support, or working out some strategies together. We may intervene directly, perhaps helping to coach our child or helping them to act for themselves. Alternatively, we may liaise with the school, perhaps getting things changed or alerting staff to a problem of which they were not aware.

Our interest and involvement indicates to the school and our children that we care about them, support them and value their development and learning. We can help to form a vital bridge between the two main areas of our children's lives – home and school.

Parents and school together

The National Curriculum: How it affects your child

Most parents are their child's main educator up until the age of 4 or 5. Then the school takes over formal education – with the lesser or greater assistance of parents. Some parents are happy to hand over completely to the 'professionals', though they probably continue to educate in ways they may not necessarily recognise as education. For example, cooking together involves weights and volume, an outing entails looking at maps, or fitting a wardrobe embraces design and technology.

When our children attend school most of us want to know the answers to two main questions:

1 What is my child learning at school?
2 How does he or she measure up to what's expected?

In other words we want information about the curriculum – what is taught and how effectively our child is learning.

The National Curriculum

The National Curriculum affects children between the ages of 5 and 16 in all state schools (including special schools and grant maintained schools) in England and Wales. (Private schools are not legally required to follow the National Curriculum although many are embracing it voluntarily.) The National Curriculum is being phased in over several years.

The National Curriculum consists of:

- the subjects that must be taught;
- attainment targets – these are the objectives or goals outlining what children should be able to achieve at each stage of their education;
- programmes of study – these are the skills and information that should be taught for each subject at different stages;
- assessment – each child is to be assessed at certain points in their school career (7, 11, 14 and 16) to see how they are measuring up against the attainment targets.

Subjects

The National Curriculum consists of 9 subjects for primary age children with an additional tenth subject for children between the ages of 11 and 14. The core subjects are English, Mathematics, and Science. The foundation subjects are Technology (and design), History, Geography, Music, Art, and Physical education. A modern foreign language is a compulsory subject for 11 to 16 year olds. Between 14 and 16 pupils will not have to follow *all* the foundation subjects.

Religious education

Schools must also provide religious education (RE) and an act of daily collective worship of a broadly Christian character. Parents can ask for their child to be excluded if they wish.

Other subjects?

Schools can – and do – teach subjects that are not included in the National Curriculum, provided they can make room on the timetable.

Attainment targets

These lay down for each foundation subject the specific knowledge, skills and understanding at ten different levels.

The ten point scale

Children's progress is measured on a ten point scale, with one being the lowest level and ten the highest. Children will progress through the scale at different rates but it's assumed an average child will reach about level 2 by age 7, level 4 by age 11, level 5 or 6 by age 14 and level 6 or 7 by age 16. However these are only averages. Some children will make faster progress and some will make slower progress. Within one class of 11-year-olds, for example, there may be a range of abilities between level 2 and level 5.

Programmes of study

Programmes of study set out the essential information, skills and processes which should be covered by children at each stage of their education in order to meet the attainment targets. The programmes of study are sufficiently general to allow teachers freedom to use their own methods and plan their own class work within given guidelines.

Assessment

In order to measure their progress through the National Curriculum each child is assessed at the ages of 7, 11, 14 and 16. Children are assessed against objectives, or attainment targets, designed to measure what the child knows. This is unlike the old 11 plus exam,

for example, which in fact measures children against each other but provides no information about what a child knows or what skills they have acquired.

Assessments are made partly on the basis of teacher's assessments and partly by 'standard assessment tasks' (SATs). In order to avoid creating anxiety amongst younger children, SATs should resemble ordinary classroom activities as nearly as possible.

The purpose of assessment Assessment is intended to indicate the knowledge, skills, understanding and aptitude which a child has acquired. In this way, assessment acts as a useful insight into what a child has achieved as well as being a diagnostic tool highlighting each child's strengths and weaknesses so that teachers, pupils and parents can detect those areas which require more attention.

Key stages

There are four stages for different age groups known as 'key stages'. These are related to the ages at which assessment is made. The stages are as follows.

- Key stage 1 from 5 to 7 years of age.
- Key stage 2 from 7 to 11 years of age.
- Key stage 3 from 11 to 14 years of age.
- Key stage 4 from 14 to 16 years of age.

Some advantages of the National Curriculum

- Because children have to follow a broad spectrum of subjects until they are 16, this should ensure a more balanced education for all children.

- Children will not be able to specialise too soon and thus close their options prematurely.

- As a parent, you will have a clearer idea of what your child is learning at school and hence be able to monitor their progress. The results of the assessments will inform you how well your child is progressing.

- Assessments should indicate a child's strengths and weaknesses, which helps the teacher, parents and child know where to target more help.

- Because all schools are teaching to the same targets, it will be easier for children who move schools to fit in with the work in their new school.

- The transfer from primary to secondary school should be easier as secondary schools will have a clearer idea of what their incoming pupils will have learned.

- There should be more continuity throughout a child's education.

Special needs
Any child who has a Statement of Special Educational Needs may be exempted in whole or part from the National Curriculum if this is contained in their Statement. A headteacher may also exempt a child from the National Curriculum for up to a period of six months, which is renewable. It is envisaged this situation may occur where a child has experienced serious illness, some family disturbance, or where a child is awaiting assessment by the LEA with a view to obtaining a Statement of Special Needs.

Reporting to parents

Parents will be informed about how their child performs in tests. Individual results will not be published and each child's results will be known only to the school, the parent and the pupil.

Other information to parents
In addition to the information you will receive about your child's progress through the National Curriculum, there are other legal requirements on schools to provide information to parents.

The school prospectus Every school must publish a prospectus, also known as the school handbook, which should be made available to parents free of charge. The prospectus includes information such as:

- arrangements for special needs;
- religious education and collective worship;
- a summary of the governing body's statement of curriculum aims;
- a summary of the content and organisation of that part of the curriculum related to sex education (where it is offered);
- the hours spent teaching during the normal school week;
- the dates of school terms and half-terms for the next school year;
- a summary for each year group indicating the content of the school curriculum;
- information about how to make a complaint about the delivery of the National Curriculum.

If you are choosing a school for your child, you will find it particularly useful to obtain prospectuses prior to visiting schools in person. Each local education authority should keep copies of prospectuses for every school in their area. These should be available for inspection at your local authority offices.

The governors' annual report to parents
Once every school year, governors are required to send a report to parents, listing the members of the governing body and reporting on the work of the governors during the year. This can include both curriculum statements and financial summaries of the school's income and expenditure.

The annual parents' meeting
This usually follows soon after the governors' report. Parents are invited to discuss the governors' report. At this meeting, parents have the opportunity to ask questions and make comments on any matters connected with the report. If there are sufficient parents present, they can pass a resolution which must be considered by the governing body or the local education authority.

Parents' evenings
Most schools hold meetings in which parents

can visit the school to look at the children's work and talk to the teacher about their own child's progress.

Parents can, of course, talk to the school whenever they feel anxious about their child. Usually it's advisable to write in advance or telephone to arrange an appointment.

School records

Records are kept on every child. These must be updated annually. Under the Education (School Records) Regulations 1989, parents and young people over the age of 16 have a right to see their records. This right of access only applies to written records – information stored on computers is covered by the Data Protection Act.

Should a school refuse access to a child's records, parents must make a written request to the governors and the governors must make the records available within 15 school days. Parents can ask for the records to be changed or for their comments to be added if they believe the record is inaccurate or misleading.

Does your child's school make you welcome?

Most schools say they welcome parents, but in reality there may be a gulf between the

sentiments and the practice. Some schools are definitely more active than others in involving parents in the life of the school and in their children's education. Below are some examples of good practice adopted by some schools. It's unlikely, of course, that any school will use ALL these measures, but there is food for thought here if you are either choosing a school or if you want to suggest some improvements in your child's existing school.

Is there a welcome on the mat?

Now that schools are more conscious of having to 'sell' themselves, first impressions may begin with the school brochure. Does this make any reference to the importance the school attaches to the home school partnership?

Do you feel instantly welcome when you go into the school? Are the following in evidence:

- a sign to welcome visitors;
- a notice introducing you to the school personnel;
- a sign indicating the school reception area;
- larger secondary schools may have a rota of students on standby to welcome visitors and accompany them to appropriate rooms;
- a parents' notice board in the entrance hall;
- children's work on display in the entrance and along the corridors, showing the school values children's efforts and takes a pride in their achievements?

Talking together

The more parents and teachers can talk to each other informally, the more they can build up trust and resolve minor problems before they turn into major ones. In addition to formal parents' evenings, many schools (especially primary schools) attempt to involve parents in the life and work of the school in the following ways:

- An active PTA which doesn't just have a fund-raising function but which also debates and discusses real educational issues.
- A weekly assembly with a crèche provided for younger siblings. The headteacher may

take this opportunity to inform parents about the work of the school in the last week.

- Teachers are in their classrooms ten minutes before the start of school or at the end of the day to talk to parents who are dropping children off or collecting them.
- Parents are told they are always welcome to come into the school and discuss any matters of concern to them. If the school likes parents to make a prior appointment this should be clearly spelled out. Secondary schools inform parents which member of staff is to be contacted – the form teacher, the head or deputy, or the head of house.

Written contact

- Each child has a home-school book in which comments and notes are passed between teacher and parents.
- Booklets are written for parents giving information about learning to read, early maths, etc.
- Parents are invited to see their children's school records and to add to them if necessary.
- Information is provided in appropriate ethnic languages.

Involving parents in children's learning

- Schools organise videos and workshops to explain their work to the parents.
- The school organises open days when parents can come and see a typical day in progress.
- Parents are invited into the classroom to help with reading, number work, cooking, or to play with or talk to children.
- Parents run bookshops, the school library or computer rooms.
- Parents are asked to help their children's learning at home and are given clear guidelines on what to do.

- Workshops are run to explain particular aspects of the curriculum to parents.

- The school organises evenings when parents can come and see their child's work and talk to the teachers. Ideally these interviews should be private. It is inhibiting for both the teacher and parents to discuss a child's educational or social problems if other people are in the room.

beginning of every academic year brings fresh challenges as children move up to a new class and have to adapt to a new teacher and sometimes to new classmates. The transfer from primary to secondary school is another significant landmark, when children make the uncomfortable transition from being large fish in a small pond to becoming small fry again. Children vary in their ability to adapt to new situations, but most experience some stress at these key times and need help and support from parents.

New beginnings

Starting school for the first time makes many emotional, physical and educational demands on children – and their parents – but the

Starting school

Playgroup or nursery school can prepare a child for the transition between home and school, by providing opportunities for children to socialise with others away from parents. But

even with the benefit of these experiences, children still have to adjust to new demands when they enter school. Many find the following aspects of school a problem.

- Separating from home. Even for the child who has previously attended playgroup the school day is usually longer and children may miss their family.

- A lower adult/child ratio: most pre-school organisations require a ratio of approximately one adult to every eight children. In school a child may be amongst 20 to 30 other children with just one teacher. This means the child receives less attention and experiences the frustration of waiting until the teacher is available instead of getting help at just the minute they need it.

- Larger premises can be intimidating and children worry about whether they will get lost, where to hang their coats, and where the toilets are.

- An unfamiliar regime can make a child feel insecure. New subjects and unfamiliar vocabulary like, 'Line up' . . . 'PE' . . . 'assembly' . . . make children feel helpless.

- Lunchtimes and playtimes can be particularly traumatic for young children who may feel overwhelmed by the larger children running around and who may find it hard to entertain themselves for a long stretch of unstructured time.

- Eating lunch can be a worry to children. The lunch time routine will be unfamiliar and they may worry about whether or not they like the food on offer. Packed lunches from home – if the school encourages them – can provide a link between home and school in the first few weeks while children settle down.

How schools can help

Most schools recognise the difficulties new children can experience in the first weeks and months and will try and help pupils settle down in some of the following ways.

- The school invites children to visit for half a day or longer prior to beginning school. This helps children feel comfortable in their new surroundings. They meet their future teacher, see the classroom where they will work and are shown the toilets, cloakrooms, hall, etc.

- Some schools arrange to admit new children in small batches so that each child can enjoy the benefit of more individual attention in the first few days.

- Playtimes are staggered so that the younger children aren't intimidated by the presence of a large number of bigger children. Some schools cordon off a separate playground for the reception class.

- Schools sometimes arrange for each new child to be partnered by an older child who will look after them at playtimes.

- The class teacher or an auxilliary will stay in the vicinity throughout playtimes as a familiar adult presence.

How parents can help

One of the difficulties about being the parent of a school child is that you are no longer on hand to help your child directly. Your help and support are generally offered from a distance. However, you can help to increase your child's coping skills and create a positive frame of mind which will increase your child's confidence when facing new situations at school.

Pre-school action plan Before your child starts school you can prepare the ground in the following ways.

- Make sure your child is as physically independent as they can reasonably manage. Can they dress themselves unaided, blow their own nose, go to the toilet alone, and eat unaided?

- Talk about school in a positive way, but don't be tempted to over-sell it or you'll find yourself dealing with a backlash on day two or three when school doesn't live up to expectations. Talk to your child about some of the interesting things they will do at school. Children may not want to have school pushed at them too much but a veil of silence isn't helpful. Pace your conversation according to your child's temperament: some children like to be talked through new situations in advance, while others prefer not to think about them too much before the event.

- Look at a story book about a child starting school – your child's librarian should be able to recommend one or two – this will give you an opportunity to talk about what goes on in school.

- Never use school as a threat. Comments like, 'You won't be able to do that when you get to school,' will not create a climate of optimism and confidence.

- Walk past the school at lunch times or playtimes before your child starts school so that she can see what's happening. Children with older brothers and sisters have a huge advantage because they usually visit the school on a day-to-day basis and they hear about the daily routine from their elder brother or sister.

- Listen out for any queries or anxieties about school such as: 'Where will I hang my coat? What will I do if I feel sick? How will you know where to find me at the end of the day?' It isn't educational problems that worry children but these practical everyday situations. Any worries, however small, deserve attention. If you don't know the answer, reassure your child you will find out. In time your child will learn to deal with problems independently but in these early unsettling days they need you to smoothe their path.

- When you know which other children will be in their class, ask one or two of them round to play before the beginning of term. Your child will feel happier to see one or two familiar faces on the first day.

- In the lead up to the first day, begin to organise your child's getting up and bedtimes in preparation for the school routine.

Separation

How will your child cope?
Some children find it more difficult than others to leave their parents when they start school. On the whole, children who have had plenty of previous experience at being away from home and who are reasonably confident with other people will feel less stressed than those for whom these situations are relatively new. However, children may surprise you and be either more distressed or more independent than you'd expected.

A child who is upset may be reassured if you can create an atmosphere of calm confidence, reminding her of how well she has coped with new situations in the past. Children who cling to their mother and weep at the school door often cope with separation better if their father or some other close person can take them to school instead.

How will you cope?
Some parents say they are delighted to hand their children over on the first day of school. Others worry on their child's behalf: will she cope, will her teacher understand her and know how to comfort her, will she feel lonely and unhappy?

Many parents feel sad. The start of school marks the end of a particular era. Your child is taking a significant step into the outside world and there's a sense in which your lives will never be quite the same again. That can be both a gain and a loss at the same time, but we cannot burden our children with our own sense of loss. We must leave our children emotionally free to get on with learning to grow up and cope with school.

However, if your last or only child is starting school, then this might be the time to consider making changes in your own life such as starting a new course or a new job.

13

Settling down

In the first weeks or even the first term, be prepared for some changes in your child. He is likely to be more tired. School makes all sorts of new demands on his emotional and physical energies. Even if you think you have got off to a good start, you may find several weeks into the term your child becomes clingy, weepy or rude and aggressive. This is often a reaction to stress or fatigue. Try and keep the pressure low and provide opportunity for extra rest and your child will settle down again. On the plus side your new school child may become more affectionate, sensible and even sleep better.

Don't be too surprised if he doesn't want to talk very much about school. Although you are probably agog for a blow-by-blow account of what's happened, your child quite understandably may simply want to forget about school when he comes home. If you are getting 'Keep Out' signals then avoid asking too many questions. Wait until your child begins to volunteer information or you may be able to elicit information subtly by telling him about some of the things you did at school.

Take an interest in everything your child tells you. He may feel resentful if you only show an interest in how many pages he's read in his reading book but switch off when he regales you with accounts of his wonderful bunny-hops in PE.

Brothers and sisters

If there are younger brothers and sisters at home, your school child may worry about what he's missing: is the younger one playing with his toys; gaining too much of your time and affection; going on outings from which he's now excluded? Tact and sensitivity on your part can help to reduce some of these anxieties. Reassure your child that his treasures will be safe and if he misses a mid-week outing, try and offer some alternative treat at the weekend.

A new school year

At the start of every school year children experience some apprehension as well as excitement at the prospect of a different class, new work, a new teacher and perhaps new classmates.

On the one hand children enjoy the status of being older, but they may feel anxious about the forthcoming change: 'Who will I sit next to?

Will I be able to keep up with the work? Will the new teacher like me? Will he be strict or easy going?' With so many questions and mixed emotions, it's not surprising that children's behaviour is contradictory: assertive and cocky one minute, worried and insecure the next.

Some children worry about change more than others. We can't hope to remove all our children's anxieties but we can reduce first day nerves a little and help them set out with increased optimism and confidence by using the following guidelines.

● Listen sympathetically to any anxieties your child seems to raise. Let him know it's natural to feel a bit worried about new situations, but point out everyone else in his class probably feels just the same and the anxiety passes after a day or two.

- If your child is not particularly forthcoming about his thoughts and feelings, then provide opportunities by asking such questions as, 'What are you most looking forward to about your new class . . . What will you most miss about your old one? . . . What do you think your new teacher will be like?'

- Boost your child's confidence by reminding him of previous times when he was worried about a new situation (this time last year for example) and how well he subsequently coped.

- If your child is going to be separated from friends who have been in his class this year, then help him to target some new friends and perhaps prepare the ground by making contact with them in the holiday.

- A shopping trip a day or two before the beginning of term to buy some new school items such as pencil case, bag, or lunch box, can send a child off happy on the first day.

Beginners' blues

Don't be surprised if your child comes home moaning about the new teacher for the first week or two. There is often a settling down period at the beginning of a school year in which a class has to get to know a new teacher's way of working.

The transfer to secondary school

The transfer from primary school to secondary school can hold a number of anxieties for children. Until now they have probably only known the safeness and intimacy of staying in one classroom with one class teacher. Suddenly children have to find their way from one class to another and may be in contact with a dozen or more different teachers every week. There are other unfamiliar things to deal with such as timetables, learning a modern language for the first time, and homework. In addition children may be aware that public exams are looming closer. This age group is also on the verge of puberty and perhaps beginning to become more moody and rebellious.

Preparing your child

You can help prepare your child for the transfer to secondary school in some of the following ways.

- Make contact with an older child who is already at the school and invite them round for coffee to tell your child about the school. (Only ask someone who can be relied on to speak reasonably enthusiastically and not one who will spread disenchantment and horror stories!)

- If your child has to travel to school by an unfamiliar route then do a dummy run together in advance.

- Emphasise that this is a chance to make a completely new start. They are unknown to their new teachers, so encourage them to work at creating good first impressions.

- If your child is going to be starting homework for the first time then look at the section on homework on page 55.

- Many children are also worried by apocryphal stories about initiation ceremonies and reports of bullying. Put your child's mind at rest; reassure him these stories are invariably made up or grossly exaggerated and neither you nor the school would stand by if there was any question of bullying.

- When your child comes home with their new timetable, suggest they pin a copy on the family notice board to remind all of you when PE kit, etc. has to be taken into school.

- Ensure you have a close relationship with your child in which he can talk to you about his emotional problems and the bodily changes he – or she – will experience over the next few years.

Help your child to learn

Helping your child at home

Whether we are conscious of it or not, we are always involved in our children's education. When we talk, answer questions, chat about a television programme or do practical jobs together, we are passing on information or helping our child to develop their skills.

Sometimes we become involved in our children's learning in more deliberate ways. Perhaps the school sends work home for us to help our child – hearing them read, testing spellings or tables. Perhaps our child is baffled by a piece of homework and we try and work it out with them. We may help our child by supplementing school work, taking them to a museum, a library, or buying them books or equipment.

We have two main routes by which we learn about our child's education. One way is by communicating with the school and the other is by communicating with our child. We may not learn a great deal about the factual 'nuts and bolts' of education through our children. If you are lucky, your child may tell you they are 'doing' fractions, long multiplication or the Romans, but you are unlikely to get much detailed information. There always seems to be a yawning gulf between a child's version of what they do in class and the official jargon of education. Few children are likely to tell you for example, 'In maths this week I'm sorting and classifying a collection of coloured plane shapes, using my own criteria and describing how the classification of shapes was made prior to checking the results (an example from Level 2, attainment target 8, Mathematics in the National Curriculum).

However, what your child can communicate is how he *FEELS* about learning; what he enjoys and what he is anxious about. You can best keep in touch with your child's feelings about school by asking open questions such as, 'Which lessons do you enjoy most? . . . What do you like about them? . . . Why do you think you are good at that? . . . Which lessons don't you enjoy? . . . What don't you like about them? . . . Why do you think you find that difficult? . . . What would help to make you feel better about this?' This will help your child and you to pinpoint strengths and weaknesses.

Importance of praise

It's important to give praise and encouragement for the things your child does well. Too often we focus on failings and overlook strengths. In fact, the more we can help our children feel confident about their positive attributes, the better chance they have of developing these qualities.

In addition, if your child knows you take pleasure in their achievements, whether this be drawing, PE, or making friends, they feel more confident about discussing their difficulties with you. They know you have faith in them and that you are not wanting to criticise and trip them up. In other words they know you are on their side.

Talking about problems

When your child knows this, he can begin to talk about his problems more openly with you. Talking can help children clarify their problems and may help them realise things are not as bad as they thought. For example, a child who feels a failure at maths may, on closer questioning, realise he can do sums alright but is floundering because he is having difficulties reading the instructions. Or a child who doesn't like writing realises that he has a lot of ideas and things to communicate but is inhibited because his spelling is weak. Once you have located the specific nature of the problem, your child no longer feels such a failure. He realises he is not 'bad at' maths and he is not 'bad at' writing but just that he has difficulty with one aspect of the subject. What's more, you can let him know that, with help and practice, he can do something about improving his maths or his spelling. Everyone can improve with help and practice.

Setting targets

Children like to see some positive improvements and it is encouraging to set some specific goals at which they can aim. For example, if your child usually only gets half marks for his weekly spelling test, you might decide together he will try for 10 out of 15 next week and 12 the following week, and so on. It is better not to promise or expect instant perfection or to aim unrealistically high, but some visible improvement can help children feel more motivated and optimistic.

A plan of campaign

Once your child has decided on a target, you can make a plan together on how to attain it. Perhaps the child decides to ask the teacher whenever he cannot understand something in class. Perhaps you agree to both spend a certain amount of time practising the difficult

subject every week. Encourage your child to come up with their own ideas of what they can do. He will be more committed to making a plan work if he has been involved in drawing it up rather than feeling he has been coerced against his will.

A child who is struggling with reading, for example, could decide to spend an extra 10 minutes a night reading to you, especially if you can agree to make that time enjoyable by allowing him to read some of his favourite stories and by not getting cross when he makes a mistake. You may need to protect an over-enthusiastic child from setting himself an impossible plan, such as working for long periods at a time. Little but often is the best way to realise steady results.

Working together

When you work together on a problem, avoid being too authoritarian or bossy. Try and allow your child to make decisions and remember she already has *one* teacher and she may understandably object to you behaving like another teacher. Try and think of yourselves as partners working together to solve a problem.

Choose your times carefully and don't expect your child to work when she is tired or absorbed in something else.

Try and end any practice sessions on an upbeat note when things are going well. It will be easier to start the next learning session if you have concluded the previous one in good spirits.

Allow time

When helping your child, don't rush her to come up with answers quickly. Give her time to work things out. Just because the solution is obvious to you, it isn't necessarily obvious to her so don't feel impatient. Remember you have a few decades' headstart on her.

Think positive

If you find yourself criticising and feeling annoyed, then make a conscious effort to retune your mind to notice your child's achievements. Acknowledge and praise the things your child CAN do instead of picking her up on those things she cannot do. Feeling successful will help her to become more successful.

Mistakes

Mistakes are a valuable diagnostic tool which can indicate where your child's difficulties lie. We all make mistakes when we are learning new things. In fact, mistakes are an inevitable part of the learning process. Think positively about your child's mistakes – they provide useful information about how your child learns.

Whenever possible, encourage your child to identify her own mistakes. If, for example, you notice something wrong in a child's sum or written work, don't rush in to point out the mistakes yourself but ask your child, 'Are you happy about this? . . . Is there anything you're not quite sure about?' The more we encourage children to identify their own uncertain areas, the more competent they become at evaluating their work.

Try and identify something positive in the child's mistake. If it's a spelling – for example they might have spelled light as lgiht – you could point out . . . 'You've got the right letters, it's just a matter of getting them in the right order now.'

A child who is fearful of making mistakes becomes an inhibited learner. She has to play safe all the time and thus stops experimenting and pushing forward the frontiers of knowledge. In this situation, a child can no longer enjoy learning because she is both anxious and bored – she can't risk experimentation and is always afraid of getting things wrong. Learning involves discovering, trying out, and testing. A child can only take this voyage of discovery if she is allowed to take some false trails.

When you don't know the answers yourself

As children move through the educational system we often find it harder to help them. Even with younger children, we may be anxious about helping if their methods and terminology are different to ours. We fear we will confuse the issue. Whenever a child is 'stuck' and needing help, the best approach is to ask her to explain to you what she has understood so far. Listen carefully in order to pick up her language and method. In explaining something to you, children will often see for themselves where they have gone wrong. If they cannot explain the problem, perhaps there is some previous example you can look back over together.

If you cannot easily understand the piece of work in question, it may be better to spend a little time figuring it out alone rather than confusing your child by attempting inaccurate guesswork.

Become a learner yourself

There's no better way to empathise with a child's learning difficulties than to put yourself in the vulnerable position of becoming a learner again. If, for example, you take up a course in Italian, machine knitting or computer programming you will remember just how difficult and frustrating learning can sometimes be. Moreover, you give learning adult status. Your child realises learning isn't just something children do at school but it is an activity we enjoy and find valuable throughout our lives. If you involve your child in helping you by getting her to test you on your verbs, or pass an opinion on some patterns you've designed, or if you discuss with her the difficulties you have working out your knitting patterns or computer program, you help your child understand that struggling to learn is a life-long activity.

Review progress

Help your child keep a sense of progress by reminding her of what she has achieved in the last few months or even the last few weeks. Keep some of your child's earlier efforts as evidence of how she has improved. Children often feel they are getting nowhere when they are constantly struggling to master new skills. If you can help them to stand back occasionally and see how far they have progressed, then

they can be encouraged by their achievements which will, in turn, inspire them to keep trying.

Emotional hassles

In theory, helping our children ought to be easy and straightforward – after all we know them better than anyone else. In practice, many of us find the situation can easily become emotionally charged. Feelings run high and we find ourselves set on a collision course. The outcome can be lost tempers, shouting, crying, accusations, or a grim silence. Needless to say, this is not a helpful atmosphere in which to learn.

The occasional brief flare-up probably won't do much damage but regular family show-downs can do more harm than good. The child feels even more discouraged and anxious – they now suffer pressure at home as well as school. They become full of tension and

feel an even greater sense of dread at the thought of the reading, maths, or whatever it is that is causing the problem.

It is important to remember that children rarely fail by choice. It is unhelpful for us to become angry with them. A child who is failing is often in quite an emotional state already. She feels frustrated, disappointed in herself, tense, angry. She is often like a coiled spring waiting to strike out or snap when anyone tries to help her. Parents may get the full blast of this tension. It can feel like a slap in the face when you are trying to help and your child shouts at you or storms off in tears.

If we respond on the same level, yelling and losing our temper in return, then the emotional temperature escalates and our joint energies will go into sparring instead of learning. If you can manage to keep calm, you may be able to defuse some of the frustration that is flying around.

How to help your child with reading

Of all the skills our child learns, reading is the one to which we usually attach most importance in the early school years. Reading is the key to success in many other subjects, including maths, which often requires an understanding of written instructions. Naturally, we hope our child will become a good reader but it takes several years to acquire fluency.

Our children need our help and support at all the main stages of learning to read. In the first place we help them as pre-schoolers enjoy books and understand what reading is about. When they begin to read their first books, we sit alongside them encouraging, helping and explaining. But even when our child has made a significant reading breakthrough, we still need to monitor their reading to help them perfect and develop their reading skills and ensure they have access to books and opportunities to read.

First steps
Long before children begin to read for themselves, they should know reading is both useful and enjoyable. We can help them to understand that the black squiggles of print are interesting and important. Children learn about the practical importance of reading in everyday situations when we read a recipe, instructions on how to play a game, directions on how to send away for a free gift on the back of the packet, or when we read street names in order to find where their friends live. The more we draw children's attention to words in the environment, the more we increase their motivation and interest.

Reading for pleasure
Reading is not only useful, it is a source of great richness and pleasure, as our children discover when we read books to them. From only a few months old, infants enjoy sitting on a knee while we turn the pages of a picture book and talk. Later they enjoy listening to us read stories and

poems. This shared pleasure in books can continue for many years. In fact, the popularity of adult story tapes or serialised stories on the radio shows we are never too old to enjoy listening to a good story.

Enthusing our children with a love of books and stories is one of the best ways we can encourage them to read. Ideally, enjoying stories should be a regular part of a child's life. Many parents find a daily story time fits in most naturally at bedtime. Even after children have learned to read for themselves, they usually continue to enjoy parents reading to them. In any event, it seems a poor compensation for learning to read if, once children have struggled through their first books, we stop reading them a bedtime story.

Apart from the shared pleasure, the added advantage of continuing to read to our children is that we can read stories that would otherwise be slightly above their own reading and comprehension level were they to attempt them unaided. We can explain unfamiliar words and ideas and thus keep the progress and momentum of reading going.

Children can also improve their reading fluency if they follow the print while we read to them. Every parent and child will be different but you may find you can continue reading to your children until they are 11 or 12 years old. You will get through a lot of books in that time!

Choosing books
Encourage your child to select books from a wide range, including stories, poems, and factual books. Most large libraries have a qualified children's librarian who will be able to recommend books for certain age ranges and interests. Make sure your child also has a varied collection of their own books. It is often through these familiar books that children begin to crack the reading code as they link the words they know by heart with the symbols on the page.

School reading books

First readers
When your child starts school he will probably

QUANTUM PHYSICS

THREE LITTLE QUARKS

A BRIEF HISTORY OF TIME

bring books home to read with you. Some schools allow children to learn from any story books of their own choice. Others require children to work their way through a reading scheme. Reading schemes consist of a series of reading books graded for difficulty. The first books in the series usually use a limited vocabulary which is frequently repeated in order to give the child maximum practice. The books progress from simple vocabulary and sentence structures to more complex language but each book usually builds on the vocabulary that has gone before. When the child has completed one book they progress to the next one in the series.

Teachers who use reading schemes believe they provide a structured approach to reading. Critics of reading schemes point out that the language is often artificial and stilted. The stories can be boring and provide little interest or incentive to read. Schemes may also encourage a spirit of competition, which can be discouraging to slower readers who see their classmates forging ahead through the scheme while they are still struggling three books behind.

However determined you are as a parent not to get drawn into the reading 'rat race', it can be very difficult to keep your nerve and not worry if your child appears to make slower progress than his peers. The trouble is that anxiety on your part will almost certainly communicate itself to your child and he may begin to feel a failure. Reassure your child that everyone learns new things at different rates. He probably learned to walk or talk before some of his friends. Everyone catches up in the end and in a year's time it won't matter at all that he was only on book three while his friend was on book five.

The story book approach

Some schools allow children to select their first readers from any story book they like or any book from a certain colour-coded group. Teachers may colour-code story books according to difficulty, so that a child knows which are the easier ones to read and which are more difficult. Some schools don't colour-code and allow children to make their selection, regardless of difficulty.

Schools who favour the story book approach believe it motivates children by introducing them to interesting stories rather than the artificial stories of some reading schemes. Critics of this system say it is difficult to chart a child's progress when there is no structure and reinforcement of reading vocabulary.

Hearing your child read

Some schools put a great deal of effort into informing parents on how best to hear their children read. Some organise workshops, demonstrations and videos. Others will send books home with no clear directions on how to set about hearing your child and what to do when they get things wrong.

If your child's school does not give any directions on how to support your child's reading then the following guidelines will help to make learning to read more enjoyable for them.

- 'Little and often' ensures your child does not become overstressed or bored. About 5 to 15 minutes a day, depending on the child's age and concentration span, will provide regular practice.

- Sit close together when you hear your child read and create a warm and relaxed atmosphere.

- Praise and encourage your child for the things he manages to do.

- Minimise difficulties and avoid dwelling on mistakes.

- Don't leave your child struggling and floundering when he comes to an unfamiliar word. Tell him what it is.

- Help your child enjoy and understand the story. Ask questions to encourage your child to think about it. You might ask: 'What do you think will happen next? Why do you think he did that? What would you have done? Have you ever felt like that? Who do you like best in the story – why? Who don't you like in the story – why?'

- If your child has difficulty following the story then read it through to him.

- See your main goal as helping your child to enjoy books. Don't let the effort of reading mar your child's pleasure in the story.

- Don't insist your child reads to you if he is tired, ill, or stressed.

Paired reading

If you are not given any directions from the school, then one of the most foolproof ways of hearing your child read is the Paired Reading approach.

Paired reading works like this.

- You and the child sit close together with the book between you.

- You start to read the story together. When the child feels sufficiently confident to read alone he gives you a pre-arranged signal such as a tap on your knee or a nudge. At this point you stop reading and your child reads aloud alone. If he makes a mistake or gets stuck you wait a minute and then join in again until he taps or nudges you again indicating he wants to go solo. You then stop reading until the next time he has a problem.

The advantage of paired reading is that it hands over control to the child who chooses when he wants to read independently. Moreover, when he gets stuck there is no fuss because you simply join in and help him over the part that is causing difficulty. In this way the flow of the story isn't impaired. This helps to maintain enthusiasm for reading and build up a child's confidence.

Some common reading errors

When children first start reading aloud, it is important to help keep the momentum going in order to build up the child's motivation, confidence and enjoyment. At this stage, when your child makes mistakes or cannot read a word, the best thing is to tell them the word, rather than leave them to flounder and lose the thread of the story.

Later, as your children become more competent and confident it is often more appropriate to help them correct some of their mistakes and provide them with strategies for tackling their difficulties. You will need to be selective about how you help. It is off-putting if you stop over every difficulty and minor error and thus spoil the story or cause undue frustration or discouragement.

Children make a variety of mistakes as they learn to read and these mistakes provide a useful insight into what is going on inside the child's mind. If your child tends always to make the same errors, this can give useful indications about how you can target help most effectively. Below are some of the common reading difficulties your child may have in the first few years.

Substituting one word for another
Children frequently read out a different word from the one which is printed on the page. Sometimes this makes nonsense of the story but at other times the child may substitute a word which is similar in meaning or makes sense in the context of the story. An example

of a nonsensical substitution might be a child reading aloud:

'The beans came out of the forest.'
instead of,
'The bears came out of the forest.'

In substituting 'beans' for 'bears' the child has selected a word that is similar in appearance though it doesn't make sense in the context of the story.

In this situation the child should be encouraged to identify and correct his own mistake. You might repeat his sentence back to him and ask, 'Does that make sense?' He will hopefully locate his error straightaway. You can praise him for recognising that 'bear' and 'bean' look very similar. You might then encourage him to spot the difference between the two words.

Sometimes children will substitute a word that doesn't look like the one on the page but which makes sense in the context of the story. For example they might read,

'The bears came out of the wood.'
instead of
'The bears came out of the forest.'

In this case he has the right meaning – perhaps he was guided by the picture, by the context – or he may have understood the word 'forest' but he has translated it into a word that is more familiar to him.

As this error does not interfere with the narrative flow, you could let it pass without comment and perhaps return to it when the story is over. If you point out the error, you should congratulate your child for getting a close meaning but see if he can tell you why the word can't be 'wood'.

Missing words out
Children frequently miss words out, especially if their eye is scanning along the line of print faster than they can speak the words. The eyes tend to run ahead of the tongue and some words may get lost. However, if this tends to happen only at the beginnings of lines your child may be helped by having a piece of paper or card to move under each line of print. This

helps to guide the eye movements in the early stages of gaining control. You may also find that encouraging the child to slow down and relax a little helps to reduce this problem.

Adding words in

Reading entails both the decoding of symbols and creating meaning from them. In the process, children sometimes put the meaning into their own words. They may add words in because they are interpreting the story in their own way and using the phrases and vocabulary that are more familiar and comfortable to them. Such apparent mistakes can indicate the child is in fact understanding the printed words and bringing something of his own to the story.

Provided the child's additions don't significantly alter the story, it's seldom worth interrupting the flow to point out the error. You could always go back over it later if it is a recurring problem.

Reversals

In the early stages, children will often read words backwards. For example they will say 'on' instead of 'no' or 'saw' for 'was'.

If you ask, 'Does that sound alright?' they will usually identify their own mistake. Draw attention to the first letter of the word and encourage them to use this as a main clue.

Stilted reading

Children sometimes read in a very expressionless, stilted way. This is sometimes described as 'barking at print'. It may indicate the child is anxious about reading, in which case you will want to put him at his ease as much as possible. Or he may not be scanning along the line to take in a whole unit of meaning. Expressionless reading can suggest the child is failing to make sense out of what he reads.

Try and help get some understanding, expression and fluency into your child's reading by reading the story through to him first and talking about it together. You could also play 'Follow my leader'. You first read a short section – perhaps one or two lines – use plenty of expression and let your child read it after

you. This frees him from the anxiety of having to work out what the words mean and enables him to concentrate on the flow of the story.

Coming to a standstill

Children will sometimes stop either because they don't recognise a word and cannot think what it might be or because they are frightened of making a mistake.

If the word is one they are unlikely to know, or if to stop and work it out would hold up the story, then just tell them the word so they can carry on without interruption. The main purpose of reading is understanding and enjoyment. You don't want to obstruct that process by frequent interruptions.

Encourage guesswork

If your child stops because he is frightened of making a mistake, you have to ask yourself why he is so worried. Has he met disapproval from you or the teacher when he gets things wrong? In fact an intelligent guess is far more constructive than silence, so do encourage your child to have a go. Praise him for a good guess.

At the end of reading, you can go back over any words that caused problems. If there are more than a few words, this would obviously become tedious, so just select those that are most useful, either because they are in common usage or because they will recur many more times in the book.

Further practice

Once your child has become more confident, you can make reading practice fun by trying some of the following tactics.

Leapfrogging

Your child reads some of the story – a paragraph or half a page depending on how competent he is – he stops and you read while he follows with his eyes. When you stop, he takes over for another section. This keeps the story moving along at a reasonable pace without the child having to put in all the effort.

Where am I?

Encourage your child to follow with his eyes while you read to him. Stop from time to time and see if he can point out where you are in the text. Continue reading.

Story tapes

Many story tapes come packaged with a book. Children can gain valuable practice from listening to the tape and following in the book. You could make your own tape by reading a favourite story onto a tape yourself.

Encouraging independent reading

Some children take more readily to reading on their own than others. While some children always have their head in a book others need constant encouragement to read alone. If your child is one of these try and encourage him in the following ways.

- Cliff hangers. Start reading a book and stop when you get to an interesting point. Let your child take over on his own.

- Make more time for reading. Many children, particularly those who are active and interested in practical things, never seem to have space to fit reading into their lives. You might allow extra time at bedtime on condition your child reads. Given the choice between turning out the light or reading most children will opt to read!

- Review his choice of books. Does your child have a range of books he likes at an appropriate reading level? Reluctant readers may gain confidence if they are given slightly easier books that they can master without difficulty. Comics and simple adventure stories can also encourage reluctant readers to have a go.

- Family reading. Let your child see you reading books. This helps to give adult status to reading and may one day encourage him to come and sit alongside you with one of his own books.

- Talk to your child about what he reads (and what you read). What does he particularly enjoy?

Reading: Are you worried?

Educational success or failure can hang upon a child's ability to read. It's natural therefore to be concerned if our child is very slow or has undue difficulties. By the law of averages many children will be slower than others at learning to read – just as some are slower to crawl, to talk or to cut their first teeth. Most slow starters will catch and possibly overtake their peers in time. However, a few children who have difficulties in the early days will continue to struggle with reading and may eventually need special help. When your child is just beginning to read you cannot be certain whether slowness and difficulties indicate he simply needs a little longer than some of his peers or whether he may be exhibiting signs of a longer term reading problem.

If you are worried, discuss any anxieties with your child's teacher in the first place. Outline the problem as you see it and try and elicit the following information.

- How does my child compare with the rest of the class?
- What is his or her reading age?
- What in particular is he finding difficult about reading?
- What can you and the school do to give him the appropriate kind of help?

You should be able to leave any such meeting with a sense that the teacher understands your child's particular problem and that you have some practical strategies for helping him. You might also agree on a period of time – perhaps a month – when you will meet again to monitor progress. In this way you ensure that you keep your child's progress constantly under review.

Teachers will sometimes tell you, 'He just needs more time.' Often this is an accurate diagnosis but parents may spot a problem before it is fully recognised by the school. Many slow starters often make a significant breakthrough at about the age of seven, but if your seven year-old is still struggling and you are worried then you may want to take things further.

Have your child assessed

You can ask the school to arrange for an educational psychologist to assess your child. (You can also ask your GP to arrange this but, as the school will have to implement any suggestions of the educational psychologist, it probably makes more sense to work through the school.) The psychologist will give your child various tests and will suggest what extra help should be given if necessary.

Could your child be dyslexic?

If your child seems to experience greater difficulty with reading than his peers, or if there seems to be mismatch between the child's general intelligence and his ability to master reading, it may be that your child is dyslexic. Some estimates suggest that about ten percent of children exhibit dyslexic tendencies while about four percent are fairly seriously affected – this is at least one in every class. Boys are between five and seven times more likely than girls to be affected and it is very often an inherited problem.

There are varying levels of dyslexia, from a very mild tendency, which may only be apparent to an expert or a psychologist, to severe cases which may result in illiteracy. Dyslexia is not a reflection on a child's intelligence, although it is perhaps easier to recognise in intelligent children when the child's general high performance in other areas is so obviously at odds with his low performance in reading. On the other hand, an intelligent child with mild dyslexic tendencies may often devise strategies for overcoming his problem with the result that they are not detected.

What is dyslexia?
The word dyslexia comes from the Greek meaning, 'difficulty with reading or writing'. Experts cannot entirely agree on its cause but it is often thought to be the result of inefficient connections between the left and right hand sides of the brain. Some people believe it is caused by faulty eye movements and can be corrected by special glasses or tinted lenses.

How to recognise dyslexia
No two dyslexics will have exactly the same problems but there are recognised groups of symptoms. If your child suffers to a greater extent than his peers from several of the following problems then he *may* have dyslexic tendencies.

Does he:

- read slowly with little appreciation of rhythm or pitch?
- frequently miss out a chunk of text or read the same passage twice?
- easily lose his place in a page of print?
- become confused about directions – left, right, top and bottom?
- have a poor sense of time, often uncertain whether it is morning or afternoon?
- have difficulty remembering sequences like the days of the week and months of the year?
- find it difficult to remember more than three numbers and repeat them in correct sequence?
- have difficulty remembering complex instructions?
- have a short term memory – he forgets things very quickly?
- have difficulty in organising himself?

- have difficulty with spelling or tend to write letters and words back to front?

Dyslexia or specific learning difficulties
Some schools will not use the term dyslexia but will refer instead to 'specific learning difficulties' (SLD). It really does not matter what label is attached to the problem, just as long as some appropriate help is given.

The emotional difficulties
Children who are dyslexic can become discouraged and demotivated. They become frustrated, they switch off at school and may have behaviour problems. This failure, which is beyond their control, is both humiliating and painful. They know they have difficulties and sense they are different in some way from other children. They often fear they are stupid. Their parents and teachers may think they are lazy or not trying. It can be a great relief for these children to understand their slowness to read is not a reflection on their intelligence or their character. Parents have an important part to play in encouraging their child and boosting their confidence and self-esteem.

Assessment
If you suspect your child is dyslexic you can:

- Ask the headteacher to arrange for an assessment to be made by an educational psychologist.

- Arrange to have your child assessed privately (the British Dyslexia Association will be able to advise. See address on page 80).

- Ask your family doctor if there are any clinics in the area for children with learning difficulties and ask for a referral.

- Contact your local Dyslexia Association and use the expertise of other local parents. (The BDA will give you the address of your local group.)

The 1981 Education Act requires local authorities to provide special help for children who have special educational needs. You can ask to have your child assessed. This often takes many months but it should ensure a child with serious difficulties receives additional tuition.

The good news
Dyslexics can be helped to overcome their difficulties by structured and patient teaching. They may find they have to work a little harder than their peers, but they can get there in the end. Many people with dyslexic tendencies excel in their chosen careers. Many do particularly well in jobs which involve spatial skills such as engineering, architecture and surgery.

Spelling

Many of us can identify with Winnie the Pooh when he said, 'My spelling is Wobbly. It's good spelling but it Wobbles and the letters get in the wrong place.' Even adults are rarely one hundred percent confident when it comes to spelling. Children obviously experience far greater difficulty.

When you look at the irregularities of English spelling it isn't surprising we have problems. Take the 'oo' sound for example. There are at least ten different ways of making it: who, woo, through, fruit, flew, Sioux, true, two, you and Pooh. Phew! Just to confuse things further think of the letters 'ough'. This configuration of four letters can make different sounds in different words: tough, though, through, bough, borough, fought.

Why spelling is important
Regardless of the difficulties, correct spelling is important. Incorrect spelling can:

- Let the writer down, giving an impression of stupidity or carelessness.
- Cause confusion and lack of clarity.
- Distract the reader from the content of the communication.
- Imply lack of care or respect by the writer towards the reader.

Children's writing naturally contains many spelling mistakes while they are learning. It is important for teachers and parents to get the right balance between encouraging children to express themselves vividly and to spell accurately. If we place too much emphasis on accurate spelling we can inhibit children's language development. They will opt for simple vocabulary which they can spell correctly rather than risk more imaginative but difficult words. For example a child may want to write

'The sea hurled pebbles roughly onto the
    beach,'
but instead write,
'The sea came in fast.'

Vividness and imagination are sacrificed to accuracy and this is a great loss.

Some fortunate children pick up spelling fairly effortlessly, but for others it is always a slog. They will seem to take two steps forward and one backwards. Often they will learn a word with great difficulty one week, only to have forgotten it the next. (Children with dyslexic tendencies are likely to experience problems with spelling too.) It is a myth that good readers are necessarily good spellers. Quite often competent readers can skim so quickly they do not register spellings.

Spelling and school
Teachers will handle spelling in different ways. Some:

- Have regular class spelling lessons. There is usually some theme behind the words selected. They may be linked to a class project or perhaps have a common spelling pattern.
- Give a weekly list of spellings to be learned and tested at the end of the week.
- Mark spelling mistakes on children's individual work and expect them to write the correct word three times.
- Ignore spelling altogether.

Uncorrected spellings
If you notice your child's work has pages of writing in which all spelling mistakes are left unmarked then do ask about this. A teacher

sometimes chooses not to correct every spelling mistake, especially in the work of a young child or one who is a weak speller. It's not hard to see the reason. Put yourself in the shoes of a child and imagine the enormous struggle you have to make to get your thoughts together, not to mention the physical effort required in writing them down. How would you feel to have your work returned covered in red ink? Next time you play safe. You don't write as much, you restrict yourself to simple words that are easy to spell. You stop thinking about what you want to say because you are too worried about making mistakes. You begin to hate writing because it makes you feel incompetent and frustrated.

As a parent you may have cause for worry if you see over-zealous marking when a child is still struggling to get their ideas on paper. This can suggest a lack of sensitivity in the teacher who isn't valuing the effort of communication behind that work. There's a very real danger the child will soon lose heart and develop negative feelings about themselves as a writer.

Parents must also be concerned if they see *no* evidence of mistakes being corrected. Children are not fools. They know they don't get things right all the time. They want to learn how to make their work better. Moreover allowing children to keep repeating the same mistakes means wrong spellings are constantly reinforced. But because you see no evidence of spelling corrections on some pieces of work you can't assume spelling is not being taught. The teacher may be taking note of mistakes and dealing with them in some other way in order to separate the pressure to achieve accuracy from the creative process. Sometimes a teacher may have a deliberate strategy of building up the confidence of an insecure child by temporarily ignoring spelling mistakes. You should be prepared to ask about how spelling is taught and expect evidence that some spelling work is in progress.

Spelling at home

Parents are likely to become involved in helping with spelling in the following situations:

- When you help them to learn the list of words they have brought home from school.
- When they are writing and ask, 'How do you spell . . . ?'
- When they show you a piece of writing they have done and you spot spelling mistakes in it.
- When you play games that involve spelling.
- When they are reading.

In the first place you should always try and respond positively to what it is your child is writing. Then you can give practical help. Here's how you might help your children in the following situations.

The spelling list from school
Some children will romp through these without any difficulty. In such cases it may even be worth looking into whether they ought to have a more stretching list. Other parents may view the weekly spelling list as a regular ordeal. However great the temptation to put off nasty things to the last minute, a regular short session of, say, ten minutes a night through the week is better than a mad panic the night before the test. Concentrate on your child learning three or four words a session rather than tackling the whole list at one go.

Friendlies, fuzzies and stinkers If your child feels overwhelmed by the list then look at how you can make it seem more manageable. An approach I use with my daughter is to encourage her to categorise each word in order of difficulty. She first picks out any words she thinks she can spell already. I test her and if she gets the word right she puts a tick or 'smiley face' against this word on the list. These words are the Friendlies. The list looks less formidable since some of the words are already mastered.

Then she identifies the words that worry her a bit but not too much. These are the Fuzzies which need a little effort before they can become Friendlies. She puts a question mark or draws a Fuzzy face beside these. Finally she identifies the Stinkers. These are the ones that need a lot of attention. As the week shape ☺

square ✷ ☺

rectangle ✷ ☺

triangle ☺ ✷ ☺

circle ☺

addition ☺

subtraction ☺ ✷ ☺

multiplication ☺ ✷ ☺

division ✷ ☺

fraction ☺

progresses Fuzzies and Stinkers gradually all become Friendlies.

By the end of the week our list looks something like the one above.

This approach can reduce some of the anxiety, tension and anger children feel at having to tackle a difficult task. A jokey approach also gives the child a sense of control over the problem and even the difficult spellings can seem quite a fun-challenge as she tries to get the better of the Stinkers.

'How do you spell . . . ?'
When your child is writing and asks for help, you have several options.

- Ask her to try and write the word on a piece of rough paper for you to check it.

- Call out the letters.
- Tell her to look it up.
- Tell her to carry on writing and leave a space to fill in later.
- Write it down for her to copy.
- Say you're not sure yourself and look it up together.

Which option you choose will depend on the situation. If you can't break off what you are doing, calling out the letters may be the only choice, though from a learning point of view this is the least satisfactory.

- If you think your child could make a good stab at spelling the word herself and if you think her patience will last out then ask her to try it herself for you to check.

- Looking up the word in the dictionary is only appropriate for an older child who can use a dictionary competently, but it can interrupt the flow of thought and it may be better to leave a space and check the word at the end.

- Writing the word down for the child to copy is the best response for a child who wouldn't be able to make a sensible guess or who has a low frustration level.

- Looking up the word together is a good solution if you aren't sure of the word yourself. It's also quite a useful strategy to use occasionally even if you do know the spelling. It is good for children to see adults using a dictionary. They learn there is no stigma to admitting you don't know something and looking it up.

- If you find your child is asking for spellings every few minutes it might be as well to break off what you are doing and sit alongside her for a bit. Or talk to her first about what she wants to say and write down a list of words for her to refer to.

When you notice a mistake

If your child shows you something she has written and you notice a spelling mistake, weigh up the situation carefully. Don't draw attention to the spelling first and foremost. Say something positive and encouraging about the content of the writing.

If a young child has struggled to write a letter to her grandparents, for example, it could make her upset and dissatisfied with her effort if you point out a spelling mistake. In such a situation it's better to praise the effort and the content of the letter and make a mental note to deal with this mistake later on in another context. The mistake may be in something important such as an address. You can use this as a good example, pointing out to your child one of the practical reasons why we have to spell accurately, or the postman may not deliver the letter to the right place. In general, encourage your child to identify her own errors by asking 'Are there any words you aren't quite happy about?'

Learning to spell

There are a number of tactics that can be used to help children and adults learn spellings. Some methods suit one person better than another. By trial and error you can probably find out which method best suits your child, though a mixture of methods is usually appropriate.

Try the following tactics next time you have to help your child memorise how to spell a word.

Analyse the problem

Ask your child to look at the word to be learned and tell you what they think is the difficult bit – there's usually one part that's more difficult than the rest. Identifying this helps you both to see where to focus attention. Sometimes, just analysing the difficulty helps children get to grips with the spelling problem.

Cover, write and check

Look at the word together and then ask your child to copy it. Ask the child to check she's copied it accurately. When she is happy with copying, ask her to cover the word and write it from memory. Get her to check her attempt herself. See if she can do it again a few minutes later.

Family words

Try and help children see spelling patterns and recurring letter combinations. If possible link a new word to another already familiar word with the same pattern. For example, bright is like light. (Write out both words and see if your child can think of any other ight words.)

Let your child feel confident with one family pattern before introducing a similar pattern. For example, if you are teaching words that contain 'ie', don't also teach words with the 'ei' combination at the same time. Similarly, if the child is learning words with 'ee', avoid teaching words with 'ea' until the first group has been learned thoroughly.

Sounding out hidden letters and syllables

Pronounce the word as it is written for the child to hear all the letters and syllables clearly. For example Wed–nes–day, Feb–ru–ary or bis–cu–it, thum–b. Children can be encouraged to help themselves by saying the words out in their heads like this when they have to write them down.

Memory triggers

Use memory tricks to help your child with any particularly difficult letter combinations.

For example,

The beginning of beautiful can be remembered by 'big elephants are ugly.'

To recall the one 'c' and double 's' in necessary you can suggest 'one cup and two saucers.'

You might help your child remember the difference between stationery and stationary by pointing out stationery has 'e' for envelopes.

It doesn't matter how quirky the idea is as long as it works. Encourage your child to think of her own memory triggers. (When struggling with the 'ough' letter string my eight-year old came up with the suggestion 'Odie uses Garfield's house'. This didn't mean much to me but it worked for her.)

Words inside words

Another aide memoire may be to notice where you have a smaller word inside a larger one, for example ear in hear or van in advantage.

Rules

The trouble with rules is that every one seems to have so many exceptions. However, they can sometimes provide useful guidelines. Rules are more likely to be remembered if you can help the child deduce the rule for herself. For example, if you want to teach that we double the last letter when adding 'ed' and 'ing' to words which end in a consonant which is preceded by a single vowel, show your child the pattern and see if she can explain to you what is happening.

hop	hopped	hopping
bat	batted	batting
slam	slammed	slamming

Reinforcement

Learning new spellings will be more effective if you can check back over the learning. Just because a child learns to spell a word one day they won't necessarily remember it tomorrow or next week. Practise and make a point of going back over words once they've been learned.

Make spelling fun

Use informal opportunities to interest your child in spelling.

Word cards

Cut out or buy blank cards. Write one of the words your child wants to learn on each card. Play a game where you lay the cards face down on the table. Your child picks them up in turn for you to read out to him. He tries to write the word. Let him check to see if he's got it right. If he has he keeps the card. If he's wrong you keep the card. The winner is the one who has most cards on their pile at the end.

Spellings are everywhere

Encourage your child to notice spellings in the everyday environment. For example at the tea table you might remove the jar of jam and ask your child to spell jam or apricot – whichever is the more appropriate. When you're buying petrol ask him to see how many words he can see around him at the garage and test him when you drive away.

Books of crosswords or word searches can motivate children to look carefully at spellings.

Games such as Boggle, Scrabble and Lexicon encourage spelling. So that young children, who are very poor spellers, don't become too discouraged, you could score one point for a near miss and two for a perfect spelling.

A personal dictionary

A book with alphabet tags – office stationers sell them quite cheaply – will encourage your child to make his own dictionary of difficult words.

Encouragement

As with all learning it's encouragement that is the best learning aid. Make a point of noticing and giving praise when your child spells things right and he will be much less touchy about you pointing out and helping him with problems.

If your child becomes discouraged, help him to see he's made progress by reminding him of the words he couldn't spell a few months ago which now seem easy.

Writing

Throughout their school career children have to produce written work in different subjects and on many different topics. Writing is a complex process which involves a variety of processes and skills.

- Thinking about what you want to say and putting it in some kind of order.
- Choosing the right words with which to express yourself.
- Scribing and secretarial skills – handwriting, punctuation, spelling.
- Reading work back, evaluating and editing.

The form and style of writing differs according to the purpose of the written work which can range from rough private notes, an informal note to a friend, a formal letter, a personal diary or creative writing – a story or poem. The purpose and intended audience affect the style and content of our writing. Over the course of time children begin to learn to tailor their writing to make it appropriate for the situation and the audience.

Children often demonstrate an urge to write from an early age, making pretend scribbles or trying to copy their name or form letters. If we can take an interest and be encouraging about these early forms of writing, children can begin to experience the satisfaction and pride that come from written communication.

Writing at home

You can encourage your children to think of themselves as writers in the following ways.

Young children
- Provide materials for 'writing' in different situations – a notepad by the phone, shopping lists, forms from the Post Office, note books and a blackboard. Children also need a ready supply of pens and pencils which are regularly checked and any useless ones thrown away.

- Praise and take an interest in your children's attempts.

- Produce a book together. This could be a holiday diary or a made-up story.

- Draw attention to the different kinds of writing you do – writing a cheque, a note for the milkman, a shopping list, filling in forms, writing letters or a report.

- Encourage your child to dictate a story to you or to suggest a caption under their pictures in their own words. Write it down in front of them and then point to the words while you read it back to them.

- Encourage your child to add their name and a message at the end of cards and letters.

- Let your child write memos to go on the family notice board.

Older children
There are two main ways you can help your older children with their writing: discussing their ideas at the planning stage and looking over their work after the first draft.

At the planning stage you can encourage your child to talk about their ideas and help them to extend these. If they are planning an essay or story you might ask them how they will start it and how it will progress. You should, however, beware of being too pushy – the child must feel this is their work and not yours.

For an important piece of work, such as an essay, many teachers encourage children to make a first draft which they can then edit and improve. When you read your child's rough copy you may see there is plenty of room for improvement, but it's important to make some positive comments first. You might point out, 'That's a very good word to use . . . That's a newsy letter, I'd be very happy to receive that . . . I like the way you describe this person . . . It's an exciting story. I really want to know what's going to happen next.'

Help your child to be self-critical in a positive way. Ask if there are any words or phrases which don't sound quite right – how could they be improved? Do some parts of the story call for a more dramatic effect?

Only after your child is happy with the content do you need to draw attention to the technicalities like punctuation or spelling. You can ask your child to underline words or punctuation they are unsure about and go through these with them. If you have to point out some errors it's possible to do this in a way that doesn't seem like a put down.

You can encourage an older child to become an enthusiastic writer in any of the following ways:

- Buy or make a diary or journal – encourage your child to write at least a sentence a day. If you keep a diary, read back to your child some of your old entries – particularly those that relate to them as a small child and they will see how interesting it can be to keep a record of personal events.

- Make up some stories together and suggest your child writes these down.

- Look out for free offers that your child can send away for.

- You can encourage a penfriendship with another child of similar age or interests.

- If you have a computer with a word processing program you can allow your child to use this for making up and correcting their own writing.

Handwriting

Handwriting develops over many years. It starts with the toddler's scribbles and continues to develop through infant and junior school. Some children seem able to master neat and even writing with relatively little effort. Others are constantly waging a battle against untidiness, unevenness and painful slowness.

Handwriting is a vital means of communication and one by which children – and adults – are often judged. If handwriting is poor it tends to detract from the content of the work. In one experiment examiners were asked to assess the same essays but in different handwritings. The neatly written work was awarded higher marks than the same work which was written badly. Children owe it to themselves and their readers to communicate as clearly as possible. (One indication that adults too are judged by their handwriting is that many job adverts require applicants to send a letter of application in their own writing.)

As well as learning to write clearly children also need to be speedy and relaxed. The slow writer adds a considerable extra burden to her work load and the tense writer often suffers from discomfort or hand cramps which make writing a painful chore.

Most schools teach handwriting throughout the infants and lower juniors, but some children need more practice than the weekly or twice weekly lesson and they need attention beyond the age at which the school provides instruction. Sometimes reasonably able writers begin to slip backwards and get into bad habits. This often occurs in secondary school when children are under greater pressure to write notes and produce more written work at greater speed.

Whether your child is beginning to write or whether she is just wanting to improve her handwriting try and help in the following ways.

Motivation

Help motivate your child to change or improve her writing by discussing the advantages of a legible and attractive script. Improvement will require considerable practice and patience on her part, so your child will need plenty of incentive to make the necessary effort. Help her to appraise her own writing. Reassure her that with practice she really can make an effective improvement.

A correct position

Make sure your child sits at a table with the chair at a comfortable height. The paper should be slightly to the right of centre for a right-handed child and to the left of centre for a left-handed child. The writer should be positioned in such a way that she doesn't block out the light or cast shadows with her writing hand.

Choose your weapon

Provide a choice of pencils or pens if your child is old enough. Pencils should ideally be soft-leaded since these move across the paper more easily. Fibre tipped pens can be helpful but check they flow easily and replace them as soon as they start to dry out or the tip becomes damaged.

A good grip

Encourage your child to hold the pencil so that it rests on her second finger and is lightly held in place by her first finger and thumb. If your child tends to hold the pencil too close to the point then wrap a large elastic band several times around the place where she should grip it.

Observe your child in action. If she has a very tight grip or presses too hard on the paper encourage her to loosen up by doing free flow writing patterns on a large sheet of paper. Examples are given on page 38.

Forming letters

When your child starts learning to write observe carefully to check she forms letters in the correct sequence – beginning and ending each one at the right place. Children can often get by with a passable looking letter which has been formed in the wrong way. This will cause long term difficulties later when she starts to do joined writing.

Which style?

While your child is still having handwriting lessons at school then use the same style to avoid confusion. Some infant teachers now teach a style of handwriting which has the tails on each letter in readiness for moving on to joined writing.

The left-hander

Left-handed children often experience difficulties with an alphabet that was designed for right-handed people. Left handers have to push the pen instead of drawing it along and they cover up their work as they progress. Left-handed children may find it easier if they angle their paper so that it tips down towards the right. Older children will benefit from having a fountain pen with a left-handed nib.

Correcting problem writing

If your child's writing is untidy or difficult to read and she is no longer having handwriting lessons at school, then you will have to work on the problem together. It may just be a

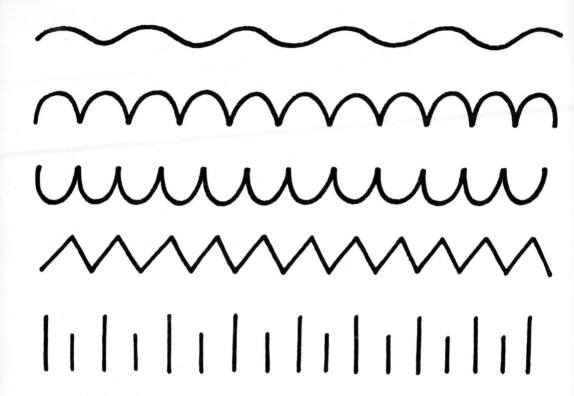

question of tidying up one or two points, or a complete overhaul may be necessary. Your child may want to improve her existing style of writing or adopt a different style altogether. This will take longer to achieve and you will need to look through handwriting books – available from large bookshops – and let her select a style she likes.

Together weigh up the strengths and weaknesses of her present handwriting. Check her seating position, grip, and letter formation are correct as already described. Then check:

- Are letters sloping in the right way?
- Are they all sloping in the same direction?
- Is the spacing between words too big or too small?
- Are ascenders and descenders (sticks and tails) too high or not high enough?
- Is each letter formed in the correct way?

Draw up a plan of campaign together. It might be a good psychological ploy in the first place to tackle something that will show a quick improvement – for example, simply making all the letters slope in the same direction will produce fast results.

Equip your child with paper and writing implements and perhaps a handwriting book. Encourage her to practise regularly. The older the child the more ingrained the bad habit will be and the longer it will take to correct the problem.

Give constant praise and positive feedback. Keep copies of early exercises to demonstrate how much she has improved over the weeks. If you feel your own writing could do with tidying up then why not sit alongside your child and work together.

Presentation

It's not only handwriting that contributes to the final appearance of a piece of work – layout is also important. Encourage your child to comment on the presentation of her work and suggest ways in which it could be improved – underlining headings, leaving a margin, and allowing space around diagrams will all improve the final appearance. A little effort is worthwhile. It conveys to the reader that you care and helps children to take pride and feel more confident in the presentation of their work.

Television

Media education – which includes the study of television, radio, newspapers, magazines and advertising – is now included within English in the National Curriculum. Television plays such an important part in our everyday lives, providing entertainment, information and shaping our views, that it's important for children to become critical and discerning viewers.

However well schools teach media education, the fact remains that most of a child's television viewing takes place within the home. One research project estimates that children between the ages of 5 and 14 spend 23 hours a week on average watching television. This is longer than they spend working in the classroom and seems a good reason to encourage children to use television sensibly and to view critically.

The good, the bad and the rubbish
Television can be both a wonderful educational tool or a dreadful time waster. How our children use it and what they get out of it depends in part on us. On the plus side, television offers a window on the world opening children's eyes to the wonders of nature and the world around them. It can introduce the very latest scientific discoveries that won't get into school text books for many years. It dramatises books which children are then inspired to read. It introduces unfamiliar cultures, opening children's eyes to different

lifestyles and breaking down prejudice. It motivates children to try new activities. It does all this more vividly and dramatically than any other medium.

On the minus side, television sometimes portrays attitudes, values, language and behaviour we wouldn't endorse ourselves. Taken in large doses it can present a distorted view of the world, encourage passivity and squeeze play and creative activities out of a child's life. It can encourage children to be acquisitive and consumer-minded.

Becoming a discerning viewer
In order to help our children use television to its best advantage we need to encourage good viewing habits. To achieve this we should

- Limit viewing.
- Select programmes carefully.
- Watch with our children.
- Talk about the programmes with them.

How much should children see?
Every family will choose to answer this in their own way but a useful starting point is to keep a diary or chart of exactly what and how much your child actually views during the course of a week – an older child could keep the diary for himself. You may find that your child watches more than you think.

Making a choice
If you feel your child sees too much television then draw up a list of agreed programmes together. Try and ensure a reasonably balanced diet. For example, are some of the following categories included – drama, information programmes, cartoons, news and documentaries, entertainment? You may sometimes want to direct your child towards a particular programme and watch with him. Of course children want entertainment and fun, but if this is all they are watching then they miss out on some of the great strengths of television.

If a child actively chooses to watch a programme rather than flicking through the channels until something catches his attention

he learns to make decisions, organise his time and be a more discriminating viewer.

Make sure your child turns off the set as soon as the chosen programme is over. We all know how easy it is to slide on into the next few minutes of the following programme and be hooked for another hour. Research suggests that what children remember from television is in inverse proportion to the amount they see.

Talking about television

Younger children will definitely gain more from television if you can watch with them explaining and interpreting the things they cannot understand. As children get older you probably can't watch all the programmes they see

(though it's worth dipping into them from time to time just to keep in touch with your child's viewing). Chat to your child about what he likes and dislikes and why. The educational potential of television is increased if we talk about a programme after viewing.

These are some of the things you might chat about with your primary age child to encourage greater awareness and more discriminating viewing.

- Which programmes do you like best and what do you like about them?

- What three things have you learned? Can you remember from the programmes you've just watched?

- How true to life do you think the characters are in your favourite drama series?

- What different kinds of programmes can you think of – cartoon, documentary, news and comment, light entertainment, quiz shows, soaps?

- How does television give us an impression about a particular character? (Or when a new character enters a series or a cartoon story you might ask your child, 'Is she going to be a goodie or a baddie? How can you tell?')

- How does television create suspense so that we're desperate to switch on again next week?

- What are some of the differences between cartoon figures and acted characters?

- Which adverts do you like and remember best (not necessarily the same thing?) Which would persuade you to buy their product and why?

- Who is this programme aimed at (ie, what's the target audience)?

- Notice media 'language' and techniques in some of the programmes eg, cross cutting, flashbacks, special effects, sound effects, close-ups.

Obviously any child will rightly resent you interrupting their viewing in order to hold a seminar on television, but well-placed comments and queries will encourage greater interest and awareness.

Be a media maker

Children learn a great deal about media by having some hands-on experience and using audio or visual equipment to make up stories and programmes. You might encourage your child to use a cassette recorder to make a radio programme. Or he could tell a story or event visually making a series of drawings or photographs. His story might be a mini drama of his own invention involving friends, family or his toys, or it may be an account of an ordinary event like 'My Journey to School'

or 'Our Trip to the Farm Park'. He will have to think about where he wants to begin and end, what he will include and exclude and, if he is taking photographs, which angles he is going to shoot from. When his photographs come back from the developers he will have to select those he is satisfied with and reject others. He will have to think of captions or a text to accompany the pictures. If you have access to a video camera, he might want to progress to making a short film.

These activities give children first hand experience in some of the skills such as planning, editing or creating special affects that are involved in making programmes or films.

Science

All children between the ages of 5 and 16 must now study science as part of the National Curriculum. If science conjures up for you thoughts of test tubes and bunsen burners then rest assured science is, in fact, related to everyday phenomena and activities which you can observe and discuss with your child at home.

In the primary years, it is possible to encourage in your children a scientific approach to thinking and observation without having access to any specialised equipment. In everyday situations you can encourage them to:

Plan and predict

By asking questions such as 'Why?', 'How?' and 'What will happen?' you can help your child to form hypotheses and to approach things in an investigative manner. For example, you might ask what happens when you hang out wet washing on a sunny day. How does it get dry? Or you might ask a child to predict which of two balls will bounce higher and to suggest why they think so.

Observe carefully

With help, young children can sharpen up their powers of observation if they are prompted to examine materials using their senses. Encourage your child to look at things carefully and to feel them to determine size, shape, weight, texture, etc. They should be able to recognise similarities and differences and to make comparisons. They should also be able to categorise things according to their main features. As they get older, children may use appropriate instruments of measurement, such as a ruler, a thermometer, or scales, to assist in their observations and comparisons.

Design and carry out investigations

You can help your child to set up simple experiments at home. For example, they might devise an experiment to find out the elements which a plant needs for growth, or investigate which brand of paper towels is most absorbent. They can find out which objects float and which sink in water – perhaps having first predicted the results. Or they may experiment with magnets to find out which objects are attracted to magnets and which are not.

Interpret results

Once they have devised and performed simple experiments, children can be encouraged to draw conclusions from their observations. For example, they may conclude that light objects float or that thin wood bends more easily than thick wood. Children should also be helped to interpret simple diagrams and charts and to use them to record their own observations.

Communicate

Encourage your child from an early age to describe everyday objects in terms of how they look (shape, colour and texture) and how they feel (hot/cold, soft/hard) as well as how they behave (things stretch, change colour, dissolve, etc). Children should also be able to give an account of changes that occur over a period of time, for examples in the weather, the seasons, the growth or decay of a plant, or the life cycle of an animal. In addition, they should be able to give an outline of any experiment they carry out, selecting the main points in a logical sequence.

The home laboratory

Here are some activities which you can carry out at home which will reinforce your child's scientific learning. Together:

- Talk about and collect pictures of living things and sort them into categories, eg fish, reptiles, birds, insects and mammals. Discuss what the animals in each group have in common.

- Sow some cress seeds on damp cotton wool and place them on a warm window sill. Sow some on dry cotton wool and place them on the window sill. Place some on wet cotton wool and leave them in a dark place. Observe and describe what happens. What might you conclude from your results?

- Grow a plant from seed. Observe and record its stages of development.

- Take note of the different kinds of rubbish you produce. Set up an experiment to observe the rates at which different materials decay.

- Apply heat to common substances such as ice, water, chocolate. What happens in each case?

- Record the weather over a period of time. Collect rain water in a jam jar in order to measure rainfall.

- Discuss meteorological symbols on weather maps. Ask your child to point out the areas where it is coldest, most windy, most cloudy, etc.

- Go around the house and make a note of all the electrical gadgets used in your home.

- Take apart an old moving toy and see how it moves and stores energy.

- Stretch some cling film or greaseproof paper tightly across a tin and fix with an elestic band. Place some sugar grains on the stretched paper. Notice how the sugar granules 'jump' in response to loud sounds which vibrate the paper.

You don't need to be an Einstein to help your child with science, but you need to encourage her to ask questions and work out solutions herself as far as possible. When she – or you – cannot work out the answers then help by using appropriate reference books at home or in your public library.

Helping your child with maths

How confident are you?

Many of us feel disadvantaged when it comes to helping our children with maths. We may have painful memories of struggling with maths ourselves and feeling a failure. In addition, we know maths has changed since we were at school and we don't know what this 'new maths' is all about.

If we lack confidence it's worth examining our attitude to maths. We can so easily give negative messages to our children without intending to do so. For example when my local primary school arranged a maths workshop for parents it was mainly fathers who attended – mothers stayed away in droves telling their partners 'You go. I'm hopeless at maths.' This lack of confidence simply isn't borne out by women's everyday experiences. We do maths all the time without giving it a second thought as we shop, balance the running total in our cheque book, compare rates of interest, check bills, calculate the material needed for curtains, measure up a room for carpeting, or estimate whether we have enough petrol for a journey. It's not maths itself that really worries us. It's the *idea* of maths that seems to cause the problem. It's important to brush up on our own self esteem, particularly if we have daughters. Otherwise they inherit from us the idea that women are inadequate when it comes to maths.

Some schools manage to teach maths in a way that gives children real concrete experiences of measurement and calculation. Others are still very dependent on pencil and

paper calculations. Parents are in an ideal situation to exploit the maths in everyday life and thus reinforce and give real meaning to the work children do at school.

Hands-on at home

Any of the following situations offer many opportunities for involving children in practical maths.

Counting

Young children learn to chant numbers long before they can accurately count a given number of objects. We can give young children lots of practical help in counting – counting the stairs as you climb up and down, counting oranges and apples, eggs in a box.

Ask your child to make a reasonable estimate of objects up to 10 and then 20. For example, how many apples on the fruit dish, how many potatoes in a bag, how many biscuits in the tin. Demonstrate how a number of objects can be grouped in different ways. For example six oranges can be grouped as $1 + 5$, $2 + 4, 3 + 3, 0 + 6$.

We can use practical examples, like putting biscuits on the plate to demonstrate one to one correspondence (ie, one for each person), or adding and taking away.

Help a young child understand the difference between odd and even. Older children should: handle money and give change; understand the meaning of a simple percentage; and make and understand a block graph. For example, how many of each species of bird visits the bird table in one day.

Cooking

This can entail weighing and comparing ingredients. For example, 100 grams of sugar looks to be less than 100 grams of flour. You can introduce the idea of doubling up or halving recipes. Children can learn about halves and quarters. You might ask them if you know from the packet that this block of margarine weighs nearly 200 grams, how can you quickly get 100 grams without using the scales? You can use

the scales to check your answer. Children can work out practical problems like how many bun cases will fit onto a baking tray.

When you put something in the oven to cook you can discuss time. If it is going to take 30 minutes to cook when must you remove it from the oven?

Shopping

Shopping offers many opportunities for practical addition, subtraction, multiplication and division. 'How many can we buy for a kilogram? . . . How much will four cost? . . . If there are six of us for lunch and we want two rolls each, how many should we buy? . . . How many six packs of yoghurt should we get to last us for three meals?

D.I.Y.

Many household jobs provide interesting opportunities for practical learning and discovery. Measuring has a real purpose when you are calculating how much wallpaper, curtain fabric or shelving to buy. Children can help you to measure walls, shelves and windows. They can calculate numbers of raw plugs and screws when you're putting things up.

You can involve them in discussing the layout of a room, working out where pieces of furniture will fit. Young children can compare distances by measuring with handspans. You may have to make a scale drawing of the kitchen together, for example, when you are planning new units.

In fact, any time you find yourself reaching for a tape measure or ruler the chances are you could be involving your child in sharing the activity and gaining some mathematical experience.

Practical calculations

There are many situations in which children can be encouraged to work things out. For example you could

- Give them a certain sum of money to shop for tea for themselves and a friend.

- Ask them to calculate the distance you have travelled on a car journey using starting and finishing mileage.

- Ask how many shots are left in the camera if you have taken 10 pictures from a 24 exposure film.

- Ask how long you will be travelling if the train, plane, bus sets off at – and arrives at –.

Calculators

Children enjoy backing up their practical learning by checking out their answers on their own calculator. For a young child a larger calculator with reasonable spacing between the number buttons avoids the frustration of pressing the wrong keys.

Activities to try with a calculator

Add up the shopping as you go round. First check the child understands place value. Ask them to add £5.50 and 10p. If the answer is £5.60 then they understand place value but if they come up with the total of £15.50, then they haven't understood about using the point.

Children often enjoy working out amazing totals such as how many bottles of milk you buy in a year, how many hours to their next birthday or how many offspring their rabbit could produce in a year.

Encourage your child to make a guesstimate of any problems they key into the calculator so that they can check they have come up with a feasible answer.

Conversation

We use mathematical terms whenever we talk about things being longer, shorter, heavier lighter, more than, less than, equal to, bigger than, smaller than. With young children encourage comparisons in everyday situations – who is taller and who is tallest, who has had more biscuits, which is the heavier bag to carry?

Helping with school maths

There may be times when we find ourselves having to help our child with their school maths either because they have brought home some homework they cannot manage alone or because they are having some difficulty and need additional practice at home. Because maths is progressive – each step is built on what has gone before – a child can find herself all at sea if she fails to understand a particular process.

If you think a stage has been missed, perhaps because of absence or because your child has not properly grasped the concepts, then it is worth talking to the teacher and asking what help you can give. Most teachers will be happy for you to borrow a workbook and will outline the best way to go over the topic. It is usually a good idea to tackle maths difficulties sooner rather than later, before your child gets further behind or begins to develop a negative attitude to the subject.

Working together

When you help your child with maths bear the following points in mind:

- Ask your child to try and go through the problem with you explaining what she *can* understand. This helps her – and you – to pinpoint the problem. Something may have gone awry in her calculation or she may not have understood a particular term or process. Listen carefully to the terms and vocabulary she uses in order to explain it to her in familiar terminology. If your child has been taught a method different to the one you used at school, then try and adjust your thinking and working out to fit the method your child uses. Don't expect her to understand a different way of doing things. That will only increase her confusion.

As she explains things, you may find your child suddenly sees where she's been going wrong and solves her own problem.

- If you are both in the dark, see if there is an example you can study.

- If you see the answer to the problem straightaway, encourage your child to think the problem through herself by asking questions which put her on the right track.

- To consolidate her understanding, work through other similar problems asking her to explain them to you.

- If neither of you can work out the problem encourage your child to ask the teacher in the next lesson. Reassure her nobody understands everything all the time and there's no shame in asking for help.

Times tables

Even in these days of calculators and computers, schools still expect children to learn multiplication facts. These are usually taught in one of two ways. Children may use a grid of 100 squares, numbered from 1 to 10 across the top and down the left-hand side. The solution to a problem is found by looking down and across to the appropriate square.

Schools who use the traditional times tables will usually expect children to learn them in the junior years. Most children need help if they are to get a firm grasp of their tables.

Here's how you can help your child.

- Initially only work on one table at a time.

- Have the table you are working on clearly written out.

- Look at the table together and see if your child spots any patterns. For example, an even number in the multiplication always produces an even number in the answer. Answers to the five times table alternate in endings of 5 and 0. The nine times table always has as its first number in the answer a number one less than the factor by which you have multiplied nine. eg $3 \times 9 = 27$, $4 \times 9 = 36$. The answers also add up to 9.

- Let the child chant the table.

- When she is reasonably confident dot around asking questions out of sequence.

- Once she is very secure in her knowledge of her tables you can begin to ask division sums. How many 8s in 32? How many 5s in 35?

- You can buy musical tapes of times tables. These may make learning more fun and are ideal for singing along in the car but you will still need to reinforce the learning by dotting around with questions.

Home and school: keeping in touch

Parents and schools together

Parents and schools need to keep in touch, understand and communicate with each other if the child in the middle is going to get the best help. In addition to the occasions when parents are invited into the school to attend general school activities, schools provide opportunities to communicate with parents and exchange information on an individual basis about the progress of each child. Parents' evenings provide a chance for parent and class teacher to talk together or for parents and subject teachers to talk together depending on whether the child is in primary or secondary school. School reports provide another important means of communication. However, this is usually a one-way communication, although parents are sometimes left a space to add their comments on some report forms.

Parents' evenings

Parents' evenings provide us with an opportunity to spend some time with our child's teacher, both giving and receiving views on our child's educational and social progress. This is an ideal time to raise those little queries which have been niggling away but which perhaps didn't justify a separate visit to the school. It's quite helpful to prepare for parents' evenings a week or so in advance by asking your child about various aspects of his work: What has he done in English this term? What kind of sums is he doing – does he understand them? Does he enjoy science – what does he find easy or difficult? How often does he use the computer?

Make a note of any queries and take it with you – it's all too easy to forget things during a short interview. If there have been some things your child has particularly enjoyed don't forget to make a note of these too. If you only raise problems and complaints you can easily create a negative tone which you don't intend. Teachers, like everyone else, feel encouraged by positive feedback and if you can tell them your child was fascinated by the weather project or has been inspired to write poetry at home after some poetry readings by the teacher you indicate your appreciation and interest.

You may be concerned about apparent failings and ommissions in your child's education. You obviously have to be diplomatic in the way you follow these up. Take into account that you have a limited picture of the situation from your child and test out the situation tactfully with a comment like,

'I get the impression from John that he doesn't do much creative writing . . . that his maths work is always done out of a text book with no practical experience . . . that he hasn't done any work on the computer this term . . . . Can you put me in the picture?'

During the interview you should gain some knowledge about your child's strengths and weaknesses. If the teacher mentions any weak areas it's a good idea to find out what she is doing about it and what you can do as well. If you feel particularly concerned about anything you hear at this meeting, suggest you talk to the teacher again in a few weeks to see what progress is being made. This ensures your child's particular difficulty is kept under review.

You will probably want to know how your child gets on with other children. Is he popular, is he cooperative, does he make friends easily?

You may find both parents and teachers gain a fuller more rounded picture of the child after talking together. In fact, it's not uncommon for a teacher to describe a child as an enthusiastic and outgoing child while the parents look amazed because he's so quiet at home, or vice versa. If there is a big discrepancy in the way a child behaves at home and school it's worth considering whether one of those situations is failing to bring out his full potential or is inhibiting him in some way.

School reports

A written report on your child gives you further information on how he is progressing in school. It indicates your child's strengths and weaknesses and points out where improvements might be made. It is a document that can provide a useful talking point between you and your child's teacher and between you and your child.

Before letting your child see his report it can be illuminating to ask him to assess himself. Which subjects for example does he think he is best at? With which ones does he have the greatest difficulty and why? Compare his self assessment with his teacher's assessment. If there are any major discrepancies it might be interesting to work out why this has arisen: does your child underestimate himself, does the teacher underestimate him?

If there are any comments you think are unfair or vague be prepared to ask for more information. For example, if there's a comment to the effect that maths is weak in some areas you want to know what areas and what you can do about it. If the report says the pupil should work harder you need more specific information: does this mean he doesn't concentrate in class, or that he doesn't complete his homework, or that his essays are only one page when everyone else's are two pages long?

Talking to your child

Parents' evenings and school reports (and any other contact in which parents and teachers discuss a child's progress) are of immense importance to the child concerned, as you will doubtless gather by the way he stands around looking both excited and apprehensive when you open his report or return from parents' evening. The two or three most important adults in a child's life have come together with the sole purpose of talking about him.

You can use the occasion to give positive feedback and to praise what is praiseworthy in your child's work. This will encourage him to keep trying. On the other hand, you may also want to talk to him about any problems. If the teacher indicates he should put more effort into a subject then talk over with your child why he is failing to meet the necessary standard. Work out with him *how* he can improve. Vague comments like, 'Try harder . . . pull your socks up . . . do more work . . . ' don't give sufficiently clear guidelines on how to improve. Encourage him to come up with specific suggestions such as:

- Spend more time on homework.
- Check answers before giving in work.
- Spend longer on the planning stages.
- Don't talk so much in class.
- Pay attention to the teacher's instuctions.
- Parents to put in extra help.

Once you have worked out a plan of campaign together then check regularly to see how things are going. It's no good being full of enthusiasm the first week and then losing interest. Your child will quite naturally lose interest and motivation too.

Your child's teacher

A good relationship with your child's teacher is a very valuable asset. If you can talk to teachers easily and informally you can often prevent a minor problem turning into a major one. Sometimes a brief word with a member of staff can make all the difference between a child going willingly and happily to school or being dragged reluctantly.

Informal communication between parents and teachers is usually at its easiest in the reception classes, when parents often come into the classroom at the beginning or end of the day to deliver and collect their children. As children move through the system teachers may appear to become more physically remote but we shouldn't assume they are less willing to meet and discuss difficulties.

Parents quite naturally don't like to get labelled, 'fussy, over-anxious,' or 'a troublemaker' but a few words at the right time can often iron out difficulties and clear up misunderstandings. If there is something you would like to discuss, most class teachers would prefer you to make an appointment by sending a note to school with your child, or telephoning for an appointment in advance.

When you're unhappy about your child's teacher

One of the most difficult problems for parents to deal with is the incompetent teacher. For one thing, it is difficult to gather objective evidence as your information comes through your children and is therefore subjective and impressionistic. Another problem is you don't want to make a fuss or single your child out for unwelcome attention. You may also suspect the headteacher and the rest of the staff will close ranks and defend any of its members against you.

One of the best ways to tackle the problem but avoid alienating the school is to deal with the complaint in a manner that is fair and friendly. A complaint doesn't mean we need to behave in an agressive or hostile way but nor does it mean we have to be apologetic and powerless. Schools exist to promote the education and well-being of their pupils and if they are not succeeding then it's up to parents and teachers to try and change the situation.

In a primary school the class teacher is a very significant person in a child's education. The teacher can make all the difference between the child enjoying a stimulating year and making great educational and developmental advances or simply marking time. Or worse still a child with an incompetent teacher may even seem to go backwards, becoming demotivated and bored.

Every teacher has his/her strengths and weaknesses. We can't expect one person to be all things to all children all the time. Part of your role as parents is to help your children take the rough with the smoothe : to understand that Mrs X may not do very exciting PE lessons but she has some great ideas when it comes to helping them write interesting stories. Or Mr Y may be strict and keep them in sometimes but, because he doesn't stand any nonsense, the children get a lot of work done with him.

You also have to remember your child is one of 20, 30 or more in a class. No teacher can give as much individual attention to each child as he or she would like. There will inevitably be times when your child doesn't get the help she needs, when she gets short shrift or rough justice. You have to make reasonable allowances and help your child to do the same.

Problems with the teacher

If difficulties persist, your child may be suffering with an incompetent teacher and her education may be adversely affected. A teacher may be incompetent in any of the following ways.

- He is disorganised. The disorganised teacher doesn't prepare lessons. He starts projects and doesn't see them through. Children waste a lot of time aimlessly milling around or they are unclear about the value of what they are doing. The disorganised teacher creates an atmosphere of purposelessness and chaos. Few children thrive in this kind of environment. They are likely to make a lot of noise and play up. The disorganised teacher is usually unclear about his educational objectives and how to put them into practice.

- The teacher doesn't cover enough work. It's difficult for parents to know how much work their children should be doing. Moreover, as the National Curriculum places emphasis on talking, listening, and finding out, a lot of classroom time may be spent on 'invisible' activities. However, if you observe very little written work has been done this may suggest the balance could be skewed and it's worth asking how children spend their time in class. But, on the other hand, don't be lulled into a sense of false security by endless pages of neatly copied exercises. This is no evidence of real learning taking place. Indeed, it may indicate that boring and futile exercises are used to keep children quiet.

- Work unmarked. Children need feedback on their work. They need to know what is good about what they have done and they need to know what their mistakes are in order to avoid them next time. To allow a child to produce written work and make no comment on it is like leaving them in an empty room to talk to themselves. Without acknowledgement and encouragement the child becomes disinterested and loses motivation.

- Work is of a low standard. Parents naturally become very frustrated when they know their child is capable of producing work of a far higher standard than that which is accepted by the school. You have to consider whether this is a temporary situation – perhaps at the beginning of a school year teachers are revising, consolidating and checking on what children have covered in the previous class. However, if children continue producing work below their level it suggests the teacher isn't stretching them. It has been shown that teacher expectations are a significant factor in children's achievements. If a teacher has low expectations then children will oblige with a low performance. High

expectations (provided they are realistic) will encourage children to produce higher quality work. Children who are not stimulated and stretched become bored and unmotivated.

When you are pointing out the discrepancies between the child's ability and the inadequate work they are producing, try and produce some evidence of what they are capable of achieving – either from work they did last year or work they may have done at home.

- The boring teacher. This is a difficult problem to tackle since it may be closely linked with a teacher's personality and there's not a great deal anyone can do about that. The teacher may in fact be covering the syllabus effectively and conscientiously but the children are bored rigid because the teacher is humourless and lacks vitality or a sense of fun.

But there may be something about the teaching style that can be improved. Try and find out from your child exactly what happens in class. Does the teacher talk at them all the time? Do they always work from books with no practical work or class discussion? Are there insufficient resources to provide any interesting stimulus? If you can identify the omissions you are in a better position to discuss the problem with the member of staff concerned or the headteacher.

- Lack of discipline. This may seem like a social problem but in fact it becomes an educational problem. If children aren't disciplined then the whole atmosphere in the classroom is one of chaos, noise and disruption. Everyone finds it difficult to concentrate and children's work suffers.

You will know the teacher can't exercise discipline when your child frequently complains they can't get on with their work because there is too much noise or other people are distracting him; when the teacher is constantly shouting at the class or threatening them to no effect; or when you know of or see for yourself that groups of

pupils are consistently misbehaving and getting away with it.

A teacher who has poor classroom management skills is not likely to be very happy about their job – waging war with 30 or so children every day can be nothing short of a nightmare. However, if parents bring the problem to the school's attention a senior member of staff may be able to help the teacher by sitting in and observing lessons and working out with the teacher more effective discipline strategies. Alternatively, there are often courses on classroom management which the teacher might attend.

Putting things right

When something is wrong it's important to assemble as many facts as you can. Listen carefully to what your child tells you and talk to other parents as well. How do they see this problem – what evidence do they have? Obviously you don't what to start a witch-hunt or base your complaint on hearsay, but you need confirmation and evidence that there is a real problem.

Talk to the teacher

Your first step is to talk to the teacher. Don't do this in an accusing way but set out the problem clearly and objectively as you see it: 'I'm concerned to see there are only a few pages of written work in my son's books. That doesn't seem to be much for half a term's work. I'm wondering what you think about it?'

Remember, teachers, like anyone else, will feel threatened and defensive if they think you are attacking them or their work. Do try and create a positive atmosphere by commenting on some of things you appreciate and value in your child's education. The teacher may offer an explanation or he may agree that he's rather let that side of things slip and will remedy it. He may not directly admit anything but you may notice a sudden flurry of written work being done over the next few weeks and you will realise your point has been accepted. However, if you draw a blank or if change is promised and it doesn't materialise your next move is to talk to the headteacher.

Talk to the headteacher

Many parents find this a difficult step, but if you assume that the head, like you, has the interests of the children at heart you will share a common concern. Be as factual as you can. The sort of comments that should make any headteacher sit up are, 'My child has only done x pages of writing this term . . . . Work hasn't been marked for the last 6 weeks . . . The teacher shouts at them all the time and doesn't seem able to keep control . . . Eight other parents in the same class have told me how upset their children are.' If you know other parents are worried too encourage them to telephone, write or visit the school to express their concern.

A head should give you space to talk, and should listen carefully to your evidence. He or she will probably not give much away and may even feel obliged to back their member of staff, but they should promise to look into the matter. If they do this effectively you should begin to see some reduction of the problem. A school's greatest asset is its teaching staff and few heads want word to get round that staff are incompetent.

A headteacher can take a number of steps to deal with teaching problems amongst his staff.

- He or she will first want to talk to the member of staff concerned and get the other side of the picture. Straight factual evidence such as work not set or not marked can be easily verified.

- If a teacher is unskilled or weak in a particular area the head can arrange for that member of staff to receive help within the school. Every primary school should have a teacher designated as curriculum specialist for each main subject. The relevant member of staff can be called upon to assist and advise their colleagues.

- The head can arrange for one of the school's own staff training days to focus on the problem in question and the teacher can be assisted without being singled out.

- A head can also arrange for a teacher to attend a training course outside the school.

- Local authority advisers (sometimes called inspectors) can also be called into the school to advise.

- Yet another alternative open to primary heads is to arrange for class teachers to swap classes for certain periods so that teachers can complement each others strengths and weaknesses.

Approaching the governors

If however the head takes none of these courses and the problem continues, parents will probably want to approach the governors who have overall responsibility for the running of the school. As a parent you can contact the Chair of the Governors outlining the problem or you may prefer to talk to your parent governors and ask them to raise the problem at the next governors meeting. Again your case will be far more effective if you can get other parents to back you.

The Local Education Authority

If you get no joy the next step is to approach the Local Education Authority. Telephone your local office for information on how to make a complaint.

The Secretary of State

The final but very unusual step for extremely serious problems is to write to the Secretary of State for Education.

Clearly one of the main problems with tackling the issue of incompetent teachers is that it can take such a long time to get any action. First you have to allow the benefit of the doubt and wait before making your first approach. Then by the time you realise this has been ineffective more time has gone by. You speak to the head and may then have to wait while the school devises strategies for dealing with the problem. In the end your child may not gain very much from the exercise, though you may manage to improve things for the children who follow after.

When your child doesn't get on with his teacher

A clash of styles

Children sometimes experience difficulties with a particular teacher because the child's personality and learning style and the teacher's are mismatched. Some children for example thrive on a discovery approach to learning in which they are encouraged to work in groups and find things out for themselves. Others feel insecure with this approach. They prefer to have everything tightly structured and to be constantly directed by the teacher. Ideally, a teacher should be able to balance their approach to give children experience in both styles.

If you suspect your child's needs are not being met then it's worth talking to the teacher and finding out what opinion they've formed of your child's learning style and educational needs. Sometimes a fairly minor adjustment in the teacher's approach can make all the difference.

A clash of personalities

A harder matter to deal with is when your child's temperament and the teacher's seem to set them on a collision course. A creative and talkative child for instance may easily clash with a teacher who is ultra neat, methodical and very disciplined – or vice versa. A child can sometimes benefit by having some of their excesses balanced but if the differences are too extreme then the teacher and pupil may find it hard to respect each other's positions.

Sometimes dislikes can be without any obvious foundation because they may be quite unconscious. The child may for example remind the teacher of someone they know and dislike – or vise versa. However, the teacher is the adult and it must ultimately be their responsibility to make sure the relationship isn't detrimental to the child's learning.

If your child has a strong feeling about not being liked by the teacher it can be helpful to bring this out in the open in a friendly way. For example you might say to the teacher, 'Ann feels you don't like her and I was wondering if there was something about her behaviour that particularly annoys you.'

Any thoughtful teacher would want to know why a child felt unliked, so do try and work out with your child in advance what it is that is causing the problem. Does the teacher tell her off more than others or never choose her to do anything nice? Be prepared when you talk to your child's teacher to perhaps hear one or two unflattering things about your child's behaviour. Try and work out with the teacher how you can both help your child improve her behaviour.

Positive thinking

If your child doesn't like a teacher help her not to give in to negative feelings since this is likely to damage her progress. Talk to her about how everyone is different and help her see some positive things about the teacher. Talk to your child about how everyone has to work with people they don't much like at times. Think of occasions when you have had to do just that. Try and keep your child's motivation alive by explaining that education and learning is something she does for her own benefit and not to please the teacher.

Parental responsibility

Whilst you hope your child's school will be conscientious in educating them, you too have important obligations. In the first place parents are legally required to ensure their child receives full time education in accordance with their age, ability, and aptitude at school or otherwise. Most parents carry out this obligation by sending their children to school. However the 'or otherwise' clause leaves the door open for parents to educate their children otherwise than at school. If you are considering educating your children at home you would be advised to contact Education Otherwise, a support group for parents who have 'deschooled' their children. (See page 80.)

However, assuming you are sending your child to school, you need to ensure he or she is in the best state to learn. Many teachers report that even young children are tired during the day from staying up late to watch adult television programmes. Attending school is actually very demanding on children's energies and they may well need extra sleep during term time.

Extra-curricular activities

Many children seem to lead hectic lives after school as they rush off to drama club, orchestra, swimming, Brownies, Cubs, gymnastics, martial arts, tennis, netball, football, dancing, music lessons – and much else besides. Clearly these activities can enrich their lives but they can also sap energy and leave a child little time for quiet reflection, being with the family, playing or for recreation. Just because these activities are available and everyone else is doing them we may sometimes feel stampeded into constant frenetic activity. We begin to feel we are letting our child down if they aren't rushing around every evening.

When life feels like one frantic dash after another it's worth weighing up your child's

needs. A shy or isolated child may benefit socially by joining a group in which she mixes with some of her schoolmates on a different footing. An undisciplined child may benefit from the discipline of martial arts or ballet. An unacademic child may enjoy the boost to her self-esteem if she can shine at sports by joining an appropriate group. A child who attends a very formal school may benefit from creative dance classes or art and craft workshops.

Somewhere we have to find the right balance between extra-curricular activities and your child's need for some rest and play.

When children start secondary school they may be so anxious about having to take on regular homework that they give up some of the activities they enjoy. It is often a good idea to counsel a 'wait and see' approach since the child may find they can manage their special interests as well as homework. In the long run it's often a child's special interest or sport that provides them with an important emotional outlet, boosts their confidence and helps them to stand out from the crowd and offer something extra when it comes to getting a job or going to university later in their school career.

Homework

Homework is a tangible link between home and school. Many schools start sending children home with work to share with their parents from the infants upwards. It might be reading, spellings or tables to learn. Later the child may have to do more formal homework. This may be finishing off a piece of work they didn't have time to complete in class, some research, some learning or some written work. Primary schools sometimes start to give work to the top juniors as a way of preparing them for secondary school.

Children vary enormously in their approach to homework. Some are over-conscientious, putting in enormous amounts of effort often to the detriment of their social life and even their health. Others make a major drama out of lifting a school book from their bag. Many manage to get things about right – they don't

need much reminding and they work conscientiously, but don't make a meal out of their work.

Homework can quickly become a bone of contention between parents and children. Parents can feel their children don't give it proper attention and children think their parents make an unnecessary fuss. Generally, homework provides an opportunity for children to work more independently, so excessive supervision can be self-defeating, although the younger the child the more they need to be helped and monitored. It's helpful to try and establish a good working routine as soon as your child starts to bring work home. Once they're into their mid-teens you probably won't be able to stop them listening to their music or half-watching the television as they revise irregular verbs or writes an essay . . . but before the ages of 12/13 you can usually have a significant impact on helping establish good homework practice.

A place and time

Foremost in working out a routine is to decide *where* your child will work. Younger children may not like to work alone however well you equip their bedroom for study. They are often happier working in the hub of the family, perhaps at the kitchen table. This arrangement also has the advantage that you may be at hand to answer queries and offer help.

Older children may want to work in their own room. If they don't already have a desk, lamp and chair then this is the time to turn part of the bedroom into a study area. A pinboard and bookshelf would also help an older child to keep tabs on their school timetable and keep their books.

When should children do their homework? This will depend on the temperament of the child as well as their outside activities and family routine. Some children like to get their homework out of the way as soon as they get in. Others prefer to have some time to relax first. Problems arise when homework is left until the last moment when it encroaches on bedtime or has to be completed hurriedly. The question of time has to be worked out together

so that homework can fit in with family life. Some children may benefit from having some incentive, such as completing homework before enjoying a favourite television programme.

It's important to know what the school's expectations are when they set homework. How long do they expect the child to spend working every night? Do they provide a homework timetable that parents can see? How much do they expect the child to do unaided and how much help do they expect parents to give? Some schools ask parents to sign a homework book to verify homework has been done.

Taking an interest
It can be difficult to gauge how far we should intervene in a child's work. Homework is an opportunity for children to become more self-directed in their study. With the best will in the world parents can defeat that objective if they supervise too much. And yet in the early stages children often need discreet monitoring. Tactfulness is one of the most important assets when handling homework. Children feel they work under supervision all day. They don't necessarily take kindly to feeling they are constantly watched at home as well.

Take a friendly interest in your child's homework. When they get in – or when *you* get in if you're at work – ask them what they have to do and discuss it with them. If they have to write a story, for example, you might discuss their ideas. You may find you can make additional suggestions, 'Had you thought about? . . . Do you remember that time when? . . .

Try and be available to go through any work that has to be learned by heart or to look at any rough drafts before they are copied into neat.

Follow up a few days later and find out how they did in the test or what mark they got for their written work. If your child got low marks try and work out together what went wrong and how it could be improved next time. If neither of you understands the reason, then this sounds like something you or your child should discuss with the teacher. Children quickly become discouraged if they are failing and don't understand how to improve.

Some common homework problems

Homework not checked
If your child's homework regularly goes unchecked follow this up with the school. Children become discouraged if they put heart and soul into their work and never receive any acknowledgement. They lose motivation and cease to take their homework seriously.

Low standards
You may think your child's work is not of a high enough standard. You will only know for sure when the work comes back marked. Of course, by then it's too late for this piece of work but it gives you both a useful pointer to see how your child can improve next time. If you think the school isn't demanding a sufficiently high standard take up the matter with the school. It's unfair and confusing for your child if the school is telling them their work is good and you are telling them it's not good enough. They don't know where they stand when parents and teachers are giving conflicting messages.

Unrealistic demands
When your child comes home in a state because they have to find out about the battles of the Civil War or the life cycle of the cabbage moth by tomorrow, then one of several things has probably gone wrong.

- Your child has got the wrong end of the stick.
- She has known about this for several days but only just remembered about it.
- The teacher has unrealistic expectations about the books you have at home or the time you have available to do instant research.

You can be sure that these requests will always happen on the night when you have to go out and can't organise a taxi service to the library.

If your child has known about this for several days you can either mount a rescue operation and help her rush around or let her live with the consequences of her lack of planning. Although this can be uncomfortable at the time it can be a salutory lesson in the long term to allow a child suffer the telling-off or inconvenience that arises from not planning her work properly.

If the teacher is making unreasonable demands, he may have underestimated the nature of the task or the resources available to the average family.

If your child has to look up information then encourage her to research in whatever dictionaries, reference books or encyclopaedias you happen to have in the house. Is there a friend or neighbour nearby who might have relevant information?

Reassure an anxious or nervous child that she has done all that is possible in the available time. Go through with her the different avenues she has explored so that she can outline her efforts to the teacher and make out a reasonable case for herself. In addition you can let her know that if the teacher is cross or doesn't believe her you will write or visit the school to support her story. This will rarely be necessary but it does give the child extra confidence to know you are behind her.

Work takes too long

If a child is consistently spending longer than you think she should on her homework you have to work out whether she is slow or whether she is given too much to accomplish in the time. Sometimes a child will spend a lot longer than required by choice: perhaps she has become very involved in the story she is telling or she enjoys doing maps or diagrams. But if this isn't happening by choice you may have to track down the cause.

A child who is slow or over-conscientious may need to be given some encouragement to work against a deadline. Perhaps you can observe where the time is going and work out some tips on how to speed up. Ask around amongst other parents to see how long their children are spending on work.

You and your child in conflict

Homework can become a source of conflict between parents and children. Parents think they are taking a helpful interest and the child feels she isn't given any breathing space. If this happens consider whether you are being a little too heavy-handed. Discuss your worries with your child and see if she will agree to take greater responsibility.

Alternatively, you might agree on a period of truce – perhaps lasting several weeks – in which you will not intervene and the child will take full responsibility for her own work. However hard it may seem for you to ignore your child's homework don't be tempted to comment or nag. At the end of the agreed time have a truth session in which you both discuss how things went. You may find yourself pleasantly surprised – or you may not – at how responsible your child was in the time. Your child may discover that after all she quite likes some input from you, though perhaps not as much as you have given up until now. Such a discussion can lead to making more satisfactory arrangements in future.

Your child's school problems: how to help

How to help

During their school life children will deal with many different problems – educational, social and emotional. They will have to study subjects they may dislike, they will sometimes feel incompetent and a failure. In their daily contact with other children, they will experience rejection, criticism and unfairness. They will sometimes feel unconfident, shy and lonely. This sounds a grim list but of course there are many positive experiences to be gained at school: when things go well there is the learning and mastery of new skills and information, increased confidence and the pleasure of relating to and working with other children. However, the positive aspects of your child's school life don't give you a problem. It's when things go wrong or your child is distressed or unable to cope that you find yourself trying to understand the problem, offer support and help your child work out some solutions.

How your child feels about school will often have considerable impact on his life and yours. The child who is unhappy, bored or dealing with feelings of failure in school is likely to be touchy, withdrawn or aggressive when he gets home. Children don't leave their negative feelings behind them at the school gate. It's sometimes only with hindsight, when your child changes class or school and you witness a personality change, that you fully realise how unhappy – or how happy – he was previously and how great an impact this had on his mood and general sense of well-being.

When you help your children to face and overcome problems they become more confident in their ability to cope with a wide variety of situations. In addition you equip them to deal with the difficulties they will inevitably experience as they go through life.

'Can you talk to me about it?'

How often do you know something is wrong but find it difficult to prise any information from your child. You are met with evasiveness, resistance, even an outburst of temper.

There are a number of reasons why your child may *not* want to talk about what may be going wrong at school:

- Protecting their privacy. Children often feel school is part of their own private and secret world. They may feel your questions are intrusive and want to keep this part of their life separate and away from you.

- Bad timing. Children don't necessarily want to talk about school just when you ask. They may want to distance themselves from the experience or wait until they are in the mood.

- It's easier to deny problems. If a child has had a bad day – perhaps other children have teased him, he has done a piece of work badly, the teacher has told him off or he wasn't picked for a part in the class play – he may just want to put the experience behind him. The 'head in the sand' approach – it'll-go-away-if-I-don't-look-at-it – may seem a comfortable way to avoid negative feelings.

- Young children may have difficulty talking about their problems because they lack the vocabulary or insight into what it is that is making them unhappy.

- They fear your reaction. There's no doubt about it, from the child's point of view parents can sometimes make a bad thing a whole lot worse. If you don't gauge the situation accurately and make light of the problem on one hand or go over the top and exaggerate it on the other then your child is left feeling uncomfortable and wishing they'd kept quiet in the first place.

Talking it over

If your child is to have enough confidence in you to discuss their problems you have to show your willingness to listen sympathetically. Quite often you can deter your child from talking to you by jumping to conclusions, criticising or getting the problem out of proportion.

Children may need encouragement in order to talk about their problems. You sometimes sense from their moodiness, rudeness or silence something is wrong and you can acknowledge this with a comment like, 'You seem unhappy . . . cross . . . upset . . . I wonder if something's gone wrong at school today.'

At other times they may begin to hint at a problem, 'So and so is horrible . . . school's boring . . . ' If you laugh or brush the statement aside then your child will not risk going any further. If you show a calm acceptance of their opening statements you may help them feel safe enough to disclose a little more. For example, if a child says 'I'm no good at maths', or admits rather shame-facedly, 'I got 5 in my maths test today,' you might encourage him to continue by making a sympathetic prompt such as,

'How do you feel about that?'
'Were you surprised about that?'
'It sounds as if that was a bit of a blow.'

Non-judgmental prompts such as these allow children to try and work out what went wrong and come to some conclusions. Perhaps they are puzzled themselves – have they failed to learn some important new rule, did they misunderstand the instructions or have they failed to do enough revision?

On the other hand a critical or judgmental comment such as 'I'm not surprised. What can you expect when you haven't done a stroke of work? That's disgraceful.', will block further communication. When he's under attack the child puts up his defences and his emotional energy goes into justifying and defending himself rather than into exploring the real nature of the problem. If you can avoid instant criticism and blame, your child can begin to work out for himself what has gone wrong.

Emotional and social problems are often even more worrying to children than problems about work. Falling out with friends, feeling unliked, or being teased can cause enormous hurt and anxiety. If a child tell us for example, 'So-and-so keeps calling me names,' a sympathetic response will encourage him to carry on talking and to explore some of the painful feelings about this. We might ask,

'How did you feel about that?
'That must be very upsetting for you.'
'Why do you think he does that?'

An accepting and sympathetic response enables children to carry on talking in the knowledge they have your understanding and concern. An unhelpful response blocks further communication by putting the blame on to children or by belittling their problem. We dismiss a child's disclosure with comments like,

'Take no notice of him.'
'You're always making a fuss about nothing.'

This belittles the child's concern and leaves him stuck with his mixed up feelings. Parents may sometimes make this kind of dismissive response if they feel uncomfortable about the child's feelings of sadness or rejection. A judgmental response such as,

'I'm not surprised.'
'You probably asked for it.'

leaves a child feeling doubly hurt. They have to deal with your criticism as well as the other child at school.

Fact finding

Because you are not at school with your child you have to rely on their interpretation of events which is inevitably one-sided. Your questioning has to try and separate the facts and reality from the feelings and one-sided view.

A problem like low marks for the maths test, for example, is straightforward. Five right is a fact. But to make sense of this information we need to know what the total number of marks was and what marks other children received. If we learn our child has performed well below his norm we need to work out the reasons why. Did he not understand this piece of work? Was he over-confident and thought he knew it when he didn't? Had he forgotten to revise for the test?

When it comes to the question of name calling, you have to try and find out whether this was a one-off event or whether it's something that happens frequently. Is just one child involved or are other children joining in?

By building up a picture with your child you can begin to understand whether this is a serious problem of long standing or whether it's an isolated incident. You can help the child develop a sense of proportion about the incident. This doesn't mean denying the upset or hurt he feels but it may mean helping him to see that it isn't too awful and probably other people have similar problems sometimes.

Strategies

When children have a problem, be it an academic or a social one, they will feel more confident and positive if they are helped to work out strategies to avoid the situation or deal with it more effectively in future. The strategies in part develop from understanding why things went wrong.

For instance, if your child got low marks because he didn't understand the work and was too nervous to ask, then you need to work out

together how to avoid this happening again. Or if it seems your child over-reacted to name calling and hence gave his classmates great satisfaction, you can look at ways in which he might deny them this satisfaction in future.

Try and help your child to think out his own strategies by asking, 'What do you think you could do differently to stop this happening another time?' (If *you* solve all their problems, the child can't develop the confidence that comes from working out his own solutions.)

Anxiety and stress

All children feel anxious and worried about school at times. This is an inevitable result of dealing with many new experiences, learning to meet other people's expectations and living in a community. We ask a lot of children when we send them to school. We expect them to develop intellectually, emotionally and socially. But learning inevitably involves a share of frustration, fear of failure, rejection and disapproval by teachers and peers. How can children not experience some anxiety?

Some children of course seem to be natural worriers who tend to become anxious and het up at the least little thing. Anxiety may show itself as:

- quiet and withdrawn behaviour;
- aggressive and noisy behaviour;
- physical symptoms such as headaches, stomach-aches, or nausea;
- tearfulness.

What can you do if your child is anxious?

- Encourage him to talk about what worries him.

- Prepare strategies. What can he actually *do* if something goes wrong. If children feel they have a strategy they feel stronger and less helpless.

- What's the worst that could happen? Help your child think of the worst possible outcome and scenario and how he would deal with that.

- Use humour. Sometimes you might be able

to send the situation up with a touch of humour. Once your child has thought of the worst that could happen, you could nudge the scenario into the ludicrous, ' . . . but supposing you broke both legs . . . or what if the roof fell in . . . ' If this meets with a touchy response then drop it but the child may get into the spirit of things and add their own crazy suggestions which you can both play with. Plumbing the depths of our irrational fears and fantasies can help us release a lot of tension and get a problem into perspective.

- Teach relaxation. Let your child sit in a chair and imagine he is a piece of paper that is being screwed up into a very tight ball. He should tense and squeeze every muscle. (Talk him through this.) Then he flops – like a puppet whose strings have been cut. Let him practise the squeeze/flop several times. Then when he can enjoy the feeling of flopping and being relaxed, ask him to think of some peaceful imaginary place – a warm sandy beach beside the sea, a tree top in the middle of the forest. Help him to create this scene in the imagination. Let this be a place he can return to in his imagination whenever he is beginning to feel tense.

- Reduce the pressure. Let your child know he doesn't have to get everything right all the time. Be sure he knows you love and value him whatever happens and never let him think your affection is conditional upon him succeeding.

- Model less anxious behaviour. Demonstrate an attitude of reasonable confidence in your own life. If you are always anxious and worried then such an approach to life becomes the norm for the child. Talk to your child about things that worry you sometimes but show how you manage them.

Boost your child's confidence

Confidence is a great asset, enabling children to make friends, tackle new situations and deal with setbacks without becoming too disheartened. Some children seem to be naturally assured and confident while others are more anxious and uncertain although all children become anxious at times.

You can't hope to turn a shy violet into an exotic bloom, although of course children can change considerably over time; but you can help to boost a child's self confidence so he isn't held back unnecessarily. A certain degree of wariness and lack of confidence is a protective mechanism which ensures children treat unfamiliar situations and people with a healthy respect until they have tested the ground. Excessive confidence may expose a child to unnecessary risks or cause him to behave insensitively to others.

Lack of confidence becomes a real problem when it seriously inhibits a child's ability to make friends because he is shy or fearful of rejection. It can also lead to underachievement at school if the child is frightened of making mistakes or taking risks. The child who can never put himself forward is in danger of being overlooked and misses out on the encouragement and support he so desperately needs.

Before considering how to help your unconfident child perhaps you should first take a look at yourself. If you are always worrying and anticipating the worst then it can't be too surprising if your child lacks confidence and optimism. If you spray anxiety around like an emotional aerosol permeating the atmosphere with insecurity and alarm, then your child will be infected with your lack of confidence. He will not be able to believe in his own abilities and will fear failure.

How to increase your child's confidence

- Always find something positive to say about your child's achievements. Even when he fails find something to praise before you examine the failures.

- Value your child's attempt even if the result isn't perfect. If your child is disappointed that he didn't come first in the race, that he didn't get full marks for a test or that his picture has turned out all wrong, look at what he may have learned from the experience.

- Don't expect perfection from your child all the time. Children who are perfectionists can give themselves a hard time. Encourage your child to experiment. Give him permission to fail.

- Give your child independence. Learning to be self-reliant and to feel competent increases a child's sense of confidence.

- Don't dwell on failures. Nothing undermines a child more than feeling his faults are going to come back to haunt him again and again. If you keep harping on about failures your child has no chance of developing confidence.

- Help your child develop his own special strengths.

- Show you love your child and think he's terrific. Never make your admiration or love conditional on his achievements. When did you last give him a hug and tell him he's great? Try it *now*.

The unconfident child

No-one is confident all the time but, for some children, lack of confidence can hold them back educationally and socially and cause considerable unease and unhappiness.

Unconfident children err on the side of safety. They can't risk making mistakes. They therefore restrict themselves because they can't, for example, hazard a guess in science or try out a new word in their English essay. They are often reluctant to speak out in class and are overlooked by their teachers. In short they can't do themselves justice and they underachieve. The skilful class teacher will help to boost the unconfident child but in secondary school teachers may simply not have the time to get to know him or her.

Fear is usually at the root of lack of confidence: fear of seeming foolish, fear of ridicule, fear of rejection, fear of criticism, fear of not living up to standards of perfection – these might be the child's own standards or other people's expectations. It is helpful to try and work out the underlying fear behind your child's lack of confidence.

Unconfident children frequently underestimate their own ability and over-estimate other people's. They may underestimate themselves because that is part of their make-up or they may not have received enough positive feedback through their life. If parents – or others – are always critical and impatient then where is self confidence going to come from? A child's view of himself is largely influenced by the feedback he receives from birth onwards.

Look at the messages your child receives and consider how you might give more praise, acceptance and reassurance. However, if a child has received a lot of negative messages you must expect it will take considerable time to build up his confidence. If you can focus on your child's strengths instead of nagging him about his weaknesses you will help build up self-assurance in time. You should always remind children of times when they have coped well and reassure them they can do so again.

Talk to your child about how it feels not to be confident. What are the things he would like to do if he had more confidence? He might say he wants to answer more in class, tell the teacher when he doesn't understand something, approach another child whom he'd like as a friend, or try to get into the football team. If he had to rate these goals in order of difficulty which would be the easier ones? Can he plan to attempt some of these? Start with the easiest.

For example, he might decide he will ask the teacher next time he doesn't understand something. Discuss with him how he might do this and what he might say. Or perhaps he thinks he will put up his hand to answer next time he knows the answer to a question. Praise him when he manages any of these goals. From these small beginnings a child can gradually gain greater confidence and faith in himself. Nothing succeeds like success. Once your child begins to experience the positive power of success his confidence will grow.

The underachiever

As parents we are naturally concerned and frustrated if our children seem to be underachieving. As a first step we have to look at the evidence: What makes us think our child is falling behind? Against what criteria is he failing to measure up?

- Does his work not fulfil *your* expectations? If, for example, you expect to see exercise books full of perfectly written essays or pages of sums with ticks, your view of learning may not be realistically in line with education today which places more emphasis on the process of learning, talking, finding out and experimenting. A lot of education is 'hidden', it never appears in a child's exercise books. Fundamentally differing views on education between parents and school lead to confusion and dissatisfaction. Before you decide your child or the school is failing it is best to talk to the teacher or head about their educational aims.

- Is your child failing to measure up against his peers? It's not easy for parents to assess this: there are occasional clues such as other children moving through a work scheme more quickly, or getting better marks for class tests. This gives you some objective measurement which you can use to ask questions at school. Teachers and parents together can perhaps begin to pool their knowledge and observations of the child to pinpoint his weak areas.

- Is he failing to achieve his own best? The child might seem to be doing well measured against his peers but we may suspect he is 'coasting' and not achieving his own high potential. Is this because the school isn't pushing him hard enough? Is he getting away with less than his best? On the other hand are you being unrealistic? Do any of us give of our superhuman best all the time – are you expecting too much of your child?

Reasons for underachievement

If you believe your child is consistently failing to produce the work of which he is capable you have to establish the cause. There are several possible explanations.

- The school. Does the fault lie with the way in which your child is taught? Is there lack of direction in the teaching, are staff demoralised, bored? Are children allowed to get away with minimal effort? Problems like this need to be sorted out with the school.

The difficulty may lie with the child. If his work suddenly starts to go downhill with no apparent change in the running of the school then you might consider some of the following possibilities:

- Emotional distress. A death in the family, disagreements between parents, a new brother or sister, moving house – emotional disturbances can seriously affect a child's work. Help your child to talk about any anxieties and try and reassure him.

- Social problems. Has there been some change in the dynamics of your child's friendships? Has a best friend deserted him? Is he being isolated or even bullied?

- A learning difficulty. Even children who normally cope well with school work can experience difficulties. Perhaps they have been absent and missed some critical piece of work. Perhaps they have failed to grasp some key learning and they have become increasingly confused.

Your child may have a learning problem with reading or spelling. This may become more acute as he progresses through the school when all subjects increasingly depend on the ability to read and write accurately. It may require patient and sensitive questioning to uncover the problem. Parents and teachers together should be able to provide appropriate educational support or get help from an educational psychologist.

- Work getting harder. As children progress then work becomes increasingly more challenging. Or perhaps the teachers are marking more strictly as children get older.

- Laziness. Children who don't like to push themselves and who prefer daydreaming to working may need to be watched and highly motivated before they give of their best. You may be able to provide some of the motivation from home by keeping in close touch with your child's progress and working out new targets with him but on the whole much of the effort will have to come from the class teacher. Discuss with him or her ways in which your child might be encouraged to work more effectively.

- Discouragement. A child may lose heart and give up if he feels his efforts are never recognised or rewarded. If parents or teachers only find fault with his work he comes to feel a failure and loses the incentive to keep trying.

- Understretched. A child who is being understretched and understimulated may switch off and lose all interest in work. This is quite often a problem with gifted children whose talents haven't been recognised and catered for.

- Easily distracted. Is your child sitting alongside a friend or group of friends who are having a bad influence on him? This is a difficult problem for parents to tackle since peer acceptance is of such major importance to children. However if this is happening talk to your child and help him to understand he is sacrificing his educational chances. A word with the class teacher might also ensure that seating is changed.

- Lack of motivation. Children may become bored and see no point in working at some stage in their school career. You need to find out why your child has lost interest and provide some persuasive reasons why he should work harder.

Peer group pressure to underachieve

Peer group pressure can exert a subtle influence on children deterring them from achieving their maximum potential. This is more likely to be a problem of early adolescence if the teenage culture considers it 'uncool' to be a swot. Children may deliberately cultivate a low academic profile in order to be one of the gang. They play around in class, stop answering questions and make out they never do any work.

If your child has usually been conscientious this can be a worrying phase and certainly one you need to keep an eye on. In practice the problem may not be quite as alarming as it sounds. Children often become skilled at 'knife-edging' – playing up in time that has low academic importance, such as registration, but working hard in the important lessons. Despite the pretence that they don't work they continue to study behind the scenes. The trouble is this is a dangerous game. Children get into difficulties when they take at face value the boasts of their classmates that they haven't done any work.

Verbal bullying

The pressure not to work can at times become quite brutal with the conscientious child branded as a swot, teacher's pet or 'goodie-goodie'. The bright child may even find himself ostracised. At the very least life can become uncomfortable for him.

Parents have to be sensitive in supporting their children though these phases pointing out the importance of not being deflected off-course by ill-wishers who are probably motivated by jealousy.

If this happens to your child:

- Show you understand and sympathise.

- Discuss with him ways in which he can respond to jibes. How can he show he doesn't care?

- Help him to define his own goals – what does he want from life and from his education? Help him to be true to himself.

- Examine the motives of his detractors.

- Ask him if he really wants to jeopardise his future to win the approval of people who only want to see him fail.

- Help him to see, although this is a painful experience at the moment, it is only a passing phase in his life. It won't always be like this. He will find people who value him – brains, talent, work and all.

- Discuss whether there's someone else in his class with whom he can pal up to minimise his feelings of isolation.

- Is there a sympathetic teacher he can talk to?

If you know there is serious peer pressure to underachieve, discuss the problem with the school who should consider how they can create a more positive attitude towards learning amongst their pupils.

Conforming to sex stereotypes

In secondary school when girls and boys are establishing their sexual identity and becoming concerned about their attractiveness to the opposite sex, attitudes towards education may be affected. Girls may be reluctant to seem unfeminine by competing with boys in traditional male subjects like maths, science, technology. Boys may use a variety of subtle and not so subtle tactics to put girls down. Ridicule, mockery, intimidation and sheer physical presence can steer girls away from subjects they may have previously enjoyed.

Boys may also find themselves under subtle pressure not to succeed in traditional female subjects like languages, literature or home economics.

Staff who are tuned in to these issues may be able to take some counter measures, so if you feel your son or daughter is being affected by peer pressures, then take the matter up with the subject teacher or ask if the school has a member of staff with special responsibility for equal opportunities.

Your best ways of dealing with these pressures are to:

- Provide your child with a wide range of experiences from an early age. Encourage girls to be active, adventurous and develop an interest in science and technology. Encourage boys to develop their gentle and considerate side. Help them to understand their own and other people's feelings.

- Give children the self-confidence to believe in themselves. This will make them less dependent on other people's approval.

- Point out examples of men and women who have successfully broken stereotyped moulds.

- Challenge stereotyped messages wherever they come from. For example you might ask your child, 'I wonder why your teacher has told you to ask your mothers to sew on your name tapes. Why not your mothers or fathers?'

- Help your child understand that masculinity and femininity are not linked to subject choices.

Gifted children

Gifted children can experience difficulties in school if their giftedness isn't recognised and their special needs aren't met. If they are bored and unstretched they will become unmotivated and their performance may even drop below average. They may also exhibit behavioural problems, perhaps being disruptive and defiant in class as a result of constant frustration.

If you suspect this is happening to your child you should talk to the teacher involved and ask if your child can be given some more demanding work. You could also seek an independent assessment from an educational psychologist who can test the child's ability and suggest ways in which the school can meet the child's needs more appropriately.

You may want to contact the National Association for Gifted Children for information about workshops and other activities in which gifted children have an opportunity to learn and socialise together. (See page 80.)

Can't concentrate

Children who can't seem to stick at a task for more than a few minutes, or who are so intent on organising everyone else that they never settle down to anything themselves, will become increasingly disadvantaged unless they can be helped to focus more single-mindedly on their own work. The teacher will obviously deal with this problem in the classroom but you can help your child to concentrate more at home.

Whether he or she is making a model, colouring a picture or tidying a room, use some of the following tactics to help keep your child stay focused on their task:

- Work quietly alongside him creating an atmosphere of calm and concentration.

- Create a climate conducive to concentration. Don't expect your child to work with a television on, for example.

- Encourage him to establish a goal for himself. For example, 'I'm going to colour in this tiger, . . . write notes for my history

essay . . . complete five sums . . . in the next ten minutes.'

- Protect your child's activity from interruption from other family members. Give his activity status by telling the other children, 'You can't interrupt him at the moment, he's doing something important.'

Developing powers of concentration begins early so give your child a flying start and

- Provide some kind of reward at the end of a completed task – praise, a drink and biscuit, a chat or cuddle – whatever is appropriate. Encourage an older child to reward himself for a period of study with a short break, a drink, a favourite television programme.

- For some tasks, such as clearing a room, preset a buzzer to go off at a particular time. Make it clear you expect the child to stick to the job until the time is up. Don't expect too long to begin with and gradually increase the time.

Don't

- Keep interrupting the child and expecting him to break off to do other things.

- Have all sorts of distracting things happening in the background when your child is trying to concentrate.

The class clown

A role some children adopt is that of class clown. This is often a way of covering up some sense of inadequacy: the child may feel less clever than the others or less physically attractive. For example a boy who is small for his age or a child who is fat may take on this role as a way to gain acceptance and popularity.

By adopting funny antics – calling out in class, cheeking the teacher – a child may gain some kind of popularity with his peers. From that point of view clowning may be a fairly successful way of turning a disability to an advantage. It can however become a problem if the child is so busy performing he doesn't concentrate on his work or gets into trouble frequently. The other disadvantage with being class clown is that no one ever takes you seriously.

If your child is a class clown it might be worth trying to work out what problem they are compensating for. You might be able to help them develop some other ways of counteracting their sense of inadequacy. For example a small child might be encouraged to take up some sport or martial arts which would increase his sense of self confidence. If your child is overweight you could discuss his diet with your doctor and perhaps think about fostering any special talent they have to help bolster his sense of self worth.

"I don't want to go to school today"

School refusal can cover a whole range of emotions from the minor protest to hysterical sobbing, headaches, nausea, shaking and a refusal to budge. Most children go through phases of not wanting to go to school (just as most adults go through phases of not wanting to go to work). It's important to help children overcome the problem with sympathy but firmness.

The symptoms

Symptoms of anxiety about school are usually expressed by a change in the child's behaviour: listlessness, weepiness, clinging, aggression – or the symptoms may be physical: tummy aches, headaches, nausea. Don't believe, because the origin of the problem is emotional, that the child is necessarily faking his symptoms – anxiety can produce any of these physical effects. The great dilemma for the parent is to try and distinguish whether their child is physically ill or whether he is suffering from emotional disturbance. The evidence is often circumstantial: the child soon seems better once we've told them they can have a day off or the nausea never occurs at weekends. If physical symptoms persist a medical check may set your mind at rest.

Causes for school refusal

There are many reasons why children stop wanting to go to school. School refusal may be the result of unhappy experiences or anxieties about school or it may be the result of anxieties about the family situation. In this case it's not so much that the child doesn't want to go to school as he doesn't want to go away from home. If the situation continues over a long period it may simply become an habitual way of responding long after the original cause has been forgotten. Some possible reasons for school refusal are:

Closeness to a parent Separation from a parent and the familiar world of home is difficult for most children in the early stages. Even those who appear to settle down well at school often show signs of unhappiness after a few weeks or months when it dawns on them they can't go back to their old way of life any more. Children who have made the break from home and parents by attending nurseries and play groups may find it easier to separate than children who have previously spent much of their day at home.

Psychologists will often look at the child's relationship with the main caring parent – usually the mother. If a mother is anxious about her child going to school or is unwilling to let him go – even if this is unconscious and never openly expressed – the child will pick up messages that he is needed at home and will find it extra difficult to separate.

What to do:

- Be optimistic about the child's ability to cope at school and your ability to be alright without him. Say goodbye cheerfully and reassuringly to bolster his confidence. Sad backward glances or desperate last hugs communicate anxiety and fearfulness.

- Ask someone else to take your child to school if there are regular tears at the school gate. If the child's father or a close friend can take him to school this can soften the parting.

- If your child is under five (below the legal school age) then consider whether he or she needs a little longer at home and discuss with the school whether he can attend part-time.

A change in family circumstances A new baby, a death in the family, someone going into hospital, moving house, or parents going through a sticky patch in their marriage, can all have their effect on a child. The connections may not always seem very obvious, but if your family is going through some kind of adjustment at the time the school refusal begins then this may well be the underlying cause.

Change in the family can make a child very anxious. If a new baby has been born he may fear he is being displaced and want to stay around to keep his foothold in the family. If someone has died or been ill a child can unconsciously fear that someone else will be stricken and they want to be at home to keep an eye on things. If parents aren't getting on well together the child feels very insecure and is reluctant to leave home. The child may also discover that if he develops a problem such as refusing to go to school then mother and father are distracted from their arguing in order to focus on his problem and so the child's school refusal fulfills a useful function in holding mum and dad together.

What to do: Firstly try and locate the problem –

- Talk to your child about whatever the upheaval is that may be causing the difficulty. Often parents try and keep things away from children because they don't want to worry them, but children always sense when something is going on and are more fearful and anxious when they don't understand the cause. Their imagination fills in the gaps with all sorts of terrors. Allow your child to express their feelings however uncomfortable these are for you. They might want to express resentment about the new baby, grief about someone being ill or dying, and anger and insecurity if you and your partner are splitting up or having a bad time together.

Something wrong at school A child may be unhappy at school for some major reason such as bullying, learning difficulties, or he doesn't get on with the teacher. On the other hand the reasons may seem fairly trivial: he is upset that he can no longer sit next to his best friend or his regular teacher has been replaced by a supply teacher. Some situations are harder to solve than others but any problem which makes a child seriously unhappy at school deserves our attention. What to do:

- Listen carefully to the child's anxieties about school.

- Reassure him you understand how he feels and you will work out a plan together. If the problem comes up in the morning try and give him one quick strategy to help him survive the day and promise you will sit down and sort it out when he gets home.

When you have your talking session encourage your child to come up with some suggestions of things he can do and things you can do. If the problem is related to some difficulty at school then promise you will talk to the teacher and hopefully work out some way the school can help.

Physical symptoms

Ill health Children may be reluctant to go to school when they are ill, sickening for something or even run-down or tired. At these times they may simply lack the necessary energy or stamina to cope. If this persists for more than a day or two it might be worth checking out your child's health with a doctor. Otherwise, a few slightly earlier nights, time for relaxation in the evenings and weekends and a good diet should help put the child back on his feet soon.

A child who has had to take time off school because of illness is often reluctant to return and may take a while to settle down again. Having become used to being at home (or in hospital) doing as he pleases and being the centre of attention makes it hard to get back into the hurly-burly of school life.

If your child is likely to have a long absence – and any time in excess of a couple of weeks will seem long to most children – you might encourage a few school friends to drop in from time to time (providing there's no risk of infection). This helps to keep the sick child up to date with school gossip and so feel less isolated. Teachers can also suggest work that can be done at home to prevent your child getting left behind.

When you suspect your child's morning headache or nausea may be a ruse to avoid school, administer the 'thermometer test' – no rise in temperature, then no staying at home. If you do give the child the benefit of the doubt and allow him to take a day off then ensure the day is fairly boring. Don't reward him with entertainment and television and he should be persuaded it's not worth pleading ill-health.

A firm stand Whatever the cause of your child's reluctance to go to school always make it quite clear that neither you nor he has a choice in the matter. Children between the ages of five and 16 must receive full-time education. That's the law of the land.

When your child makes a token protest about going to school you can let him know you don't want to go to work sometimes. In all probability there are days when his teachers don't want to go to school either but we all have to do things we don't want to do. Be sympathetic but create an atmosphere in which problems are seen as solvable.

Tackling the problem Find out the underlying cause of the problem as soon as possible. Once a child begins to solve his problems by staying away from school he gets used to opting out of difficulties rather than confronting them and finding solutions. Moreover, once he gets out of the school routine and falls behind with his work, it becomes even more difficult to return later.

If the problem lies with the school or you can't find out the cause, then talk to staff to see if they can cast any light on the difficulty. Sometimes a change of class – or even a change of school may resolve matters.

Outside help
If you cannot solve the problem using any of the above suggestions or if your child's reactions are extreme or frightening, for example,

vomiting, screaming fits, headaches or shaking, you probably need professional help to get you both through the problem. You could contact your local Child Guidance clinic or ask the school to put you in touch with an educational psychologist.

Psychologists use a variety of methods and you may want to find out in advance what approach is likely to be used in your area. Some will spend a considerable time counselling the child or the family. They may use desensitisation techniques to lower the child's anxiety feelings about school. Others adopt a no-nonsense-get-them-back-to-school approach and may escort you and the child to school for several days or longer. You will hopefully resolve the problem before it comes to this.

Education at home

Parents who find their children seem unable to settle at school or who feel schools don't meet the needs of their children can opt to teach their children at home, but they have to be able to convince their Local Education Authority that they are providing 'efficient full-time education suitable to his age, ability and aptitude.' The home option requires an enormous commitment of parental time and can leave a child somewhat isolated. It is always advisable to seek advice before withdrawing your child from formal education either from ACE or Education Otherwise, a support group for parents who educate their children at home. (See addresses on page 80.)

Going away with the school

Many schools arrange residential trips of a few days or longer in which children go away with classmates and members of staff to a hotel or field centre in the UK or abroad. The purpose of the trip may be to study a different environment, study another language or culture, or to undertake some physical instruction such as skiing, sailing or an outward bound course.

Whatever the educational purpose of the trip, most experienced teachers observe there are important social advantages for pupils. Children and teachers get to know each other and relate in a new way. Children who may never have stayed away from their families before have an opportunity to stretch the umbilical cord and become just a little more independent.

When deciding whether or not to allow your son or daughter to go on a school trip you obviously have to weigh up several factors:

- The cost. Check whether there are hidden costs such as hiring of equipment or buying special clothing with a holiday like skiing.

- The educational value of the trip. Schools normally expect to explain their itinerary and programme of study before parents commit themselves.

- Will there be a high level of supervision by competent adults? You need to know that children will be supervised constantly particularly on ferries and outings. Are the party leaders and other adult members experienced in organising and escorting school trips? Ideally, at least one member of staff should have previously undertaken this trip and inspected the facilities in order to be familiar with any problems. If the school is going on an adventure course, will all instructors have relevant qualifications and are they safety conscious?

- Has the accommodation been recently checked for safety – particularly by fire officers? Will there be a fire drill as soon as the children arrive?

- Finally, if your child has any particular health problems or dietary requirements do tell the school at an early stage for them to decide whether they are prepared to take on this responsibility.

Homesickness
Some children will find it easier to be away from home than others, but most will feel homesick at some point in their trip and this can become very infectious. If your child is unusually quiet – or unusually bright – before he leaves he may be worrying about leaving you. Perhaps you can acknowledge with him that he may miss homes occasionally – and this is quite natural – but reassure him the sad feelings won't last. Help him to feel confident and to look forward to the interesting things he will be doing.

The chances are your child will do quite a lot of growing up in the few days away from you and will return more confident and self possessed. Going away with the school is yet another opportunity for children and parents to separate a little further in readiness for more significant departures and separations later in life.

Friends and enemies: helping your child to socialise

Getting on with other children

In the primary school and early secondary school children's friendships tend to be changeable and fluid. A child may have one or two special friends with whom they play most frequently, but for much of the time they will play in small groups with a changing membership. These frequent groupings and regroupings produce inevitable casualties with one child left out in the cold today and another one left out tomorrow. Your child will almost certainly take turns at being left out from time to time just like everyone else.

Acceptance by the peer group is of great importance to children who can feel desperately unhappy when their special friend goes off with someone else or if a group they want to join rejects them. Most of us at some point will have to help our child through a few difficult patches. Some children may find isolation a major social problem in their school lives.

What goes wrong?

Children can find themselves having difficulties with friends for any number of reasons. Some of these will have something to do with the child and some will be outside her control. Possible reasons why a child may experience difficulty getting on with others are:

- He or she is different in some way. Children are great conformists and anyone who is different may find themselves isolated or teased. Children may pick on someone who wears glasses, has an unusual name, is fat, has some disability, behaves differently, is less or more intelligent, has a different racial background, wears clothes that are different or is out of step in some other way.

- A change in the group dynamics. For example a new child entering the class, someone moving away, or a reorganisation of classroom seating can create a temporary hiatus while everyone jostles for new positions.

- A particularly manipulative, malicious child may 'pick on' your child and use his/her power to isolate her from other children. Different children are likely to find themselves in the hot seat at different times.

- The ethos of the school or the class teacher may encourage competitiveness and aggression which is unconducive to fostering positive relationships.

- A child who is undergoing some temporary loss of confidence, perhaps because of changes in home circumstances, may be particularly vulnerable to isolation.

- Lack of confidence and social skills can leave a child isolated.

- A physically isolated child, who lives a long way from the rest of the class and misses out on opportunities to play informally with classmates during weekends and holidays, may miss out on important interactions that help to hold other members of the group together.

What makes children popular?

In order to consider how to help your child get on better with her classmates, it is helpful to look at some of the qualities that account for popularity amongst children. Some of the factors that determine popularity are intelligence, ability in sports or in some other activity prized by the group, physical maturity, and social skills – the ability to initiate conversations and games and to play co-operatively.

"No-one will play with me"

This must be one of the most heartrending statements you can hear from your children. You sympathise with their isolation yet feel you can do little directly to cushion them from the pain. It is difficult for parents to deal with the ups and downs of children's friendships. You cannot see what is happening and you cannot intervene yourself. Your support and advice has to be handed out from the sidelines.

Action plan
You can help your child deal with difficult relationships using some of the following tactics.

- Give moral support. You can sympathise and let your children know you understand how painful it is to feel rejected and lonely. (You should never underestimate how distressing rejection can be – it really can feel like the end of the world to a child when she feels no one wants to play with her.)

- Provide a sense of perspective. You can help your child to think of times when other children have been left out in the cold and help her realise this is a situation which happens to everyone sometimes.

- Try and understand what is going on and why. Talk to your child and build up a picture of what is happening: who has fallen out with them? When does this happen and how often? I know of one parent who, having been told by her daughter that she never had anyone to play with at lunch times, walked past the playground the next lunch time and saw her daughter running around and playing happily with a large group. This doesn't mean the daughter had been lying – just that the situation had either changed suddenly or perhaps she had been isolated for a short time and this *felt* as if she spent the whole time alone.

- Enhance your child's popularity ratings by helping her develop special skills. She may never be an athlete or ball player but perhaps you can coach her so that she doesn't come last all the time or infuriate her team members by always dropping the ball.

- Provide opportunities to socialise. Find out what swimming groups, Brownie packs, or dancing classes other children in the class attend and consider enrolling your child. Out of school activities can help to cement in-school relationships.

- Help her to target one or two possible friends and invite them round to play at home.

- Perhaps you could organise a party for her. It won't solve any long term problems but a party can give a child a temporary social boost.

- Minimise any 'differences'. If for example your daughter is fat, can you slim her down discreetly or at least minimise her size by choosing appropriate clothes? Try not to make her wear clothes or haristyles that make her stand out from everyone else.

- Discuss the problem with the school. A change of seating, talking to ring leaders or promoting more positive relationships may help. A less popular child can gain popularity by association if she is sat next to a popular child. This might be something the class teacher could arrange. The teacher can also show her regard for the child by giving her some high status in class.

- Look at any personality traits which might be putting other children off. For example, is your child bossy, uncooperative, or aggressive? Does she whinge or tell tales? Discuss with her how she can change her behaviour, but be tactful as she is already feeling very vulnerable and will feel doubly criticised if she thinks you are criticising her too.

- Coach your child in social skills. Some children simply don't suss out the rules of social interaction as quickly as others. With a little patience they can learn to relate better to others.

Help your child become more sociable

Try and observe your child closely on some occasion when she is with another child – perhaps when a friend comes round to play at home. Make a mental note of what behaviours seem to help the relationship and what behaviours seem to obstruct a good relationship. Be very specific about your observations. Your list of positive behaviours may include:

- Offering her friend something to drink.
- Asking the friend what they'd like to do.
- Showing her friend her pet hamster.
- Suggesting a game to play together.
- Taking turns.
- Making kind or encouraging remarks to her friend.

- Smiling.

Your list of negative behaviours may include:

- Flopping around being bored.
- Not making any suggestions of things to do or initiating any activities.
- Not taking turns.
- Not sharing.
- Excluding her friend from her activities or not allowing him/her to touch her things.
- Ordering her friend around.
- Making unkind comments.
- Looking miserable.

None of us is really sure how other people see us or what it is about our behaviour that attracts others or puts them off. Although it may be glaringly obvious to parents that some of the things our child does are not going to win friends and influence people, it is not necessarily obvious to the child. We need to tactfully point out where she is going wrong and work out with the child some alternative ways of behaving. This four-point plan will help you to help your child.

1 Feedback

When you have observed your child's behaviour, ask her what she enjoyed and didn't enjoy about her friend's visit. Talk to her about what things she seemed to handle well. This positive feedback reinforces the useful social skills and increases the child's confidence. Then talk – tactfully – about anything your child said and did that might have been offputting to the other child. Encourage your child to think how they would have felt about being on the receiving end of that behaviour. Your child shouldn't feel they are being undermined, rather that you are treating them as a grownup, discussing psychology and relationships with them. You might talk to them about some of the things that make you comfortable or uncomfortable when you are with other people.

2 Positive tactics

Help your child think of one or two positive things she might try out next time she is with another child. She might decide to:

- Suggest one or two games they could play.
- Take turns at playing.
- Share a piece of news or show her friend something she has made.

Having a plan gives a child a little more confidence and makes her feel more optimistic about getting on with her friends.

3 Practice

You could try role-playing how to be a good friend and how to be a bad friend in a lighthearted way together (see page 77). When your child is going to play with a child again ask her to remind you of the plan you devised together. If the meeting occurs at your house perhaps you could keep a low profile and monitor things discreetly, ready to move in with a suggestion for a game or the offer of a snack when things seem to be flagging.

4 Review

Chat to your child about how things went. Give her encouragement and praise for any attempts she made to improve the relationship. Help her to feel philosophical about difficulties – you win some, you lose some – and you try again next time.

Solitary survival

When your child is going through a difficult patch and feeling isolated and lonely at school, work out a few face-saving tactics together to help her cope with uncomfortable situations. The following tips will help her to survive when she is friendless.

- Don't let others see how upset she is. If other children call her names or exclude her she needs to be be a good actress and pretend she doesn't really mind being on her own.

- Take something to school she can play with on her own – a puzzle, a comic, a game. This can help to disguise her loneliness and it may bring other children round out of curiosity and interest.

- If other children laugh at her, encourage her to join in the joke however much it hurts.
- Encourage her to try and smile and look friendly then other children will be more likely to want to play.

Undesirable friends

In addition to the problem of no friends is the problem of the wrong kind of friends. As parents we are sometimes less than enthusiastic about our children's friends. We may think they are an undesirable influence. Perhaps they distract our child from work or they may seem to be too dominant or even a bit weak and wimpish.

Children have different emotional needs at different times of their development and in the course of growing up you can expect to see a variety of friends come and go. At times you may be aware of an imbalance in your child's relationships : perhaps your child is the dominant one among passive friends or the weak one who plays the stooge to stronger characters. The inequality may suggest your child lacks social confidence. This isn't to say they won't eventually gain the confidence to enjoy more egalitarian friendships just that they aren't ready at the moment.

Sometimes, of course, children have to make do with the only friends they can get. Even a less than ideal friend is better than no friend at all.

Don't knock their friends

It is rarely productive to be directly critical of children's friends. This tends to make them defensive and put them in a position of conflicting loyalties. However, an occasional and gentle remark from you that acknowledges some of the difficulties in the relationship can help a child clarify her feelings. For example, if your daughter is telling you about a friend talking about her behind her back, you might observe, 'Julie often seems to run you down to

other people these days . . . that must make you feel upset.'

Teasing and name calling

Teasing can be a fairly mild kind of baiting or a chronic form of psychological bullying.

Most children have to deal with teasing from time to time. Some are reasonably unbothered and shrug off taunts and insults while others take things more seriously and probably over react. The child who can manage to ignore provocation provides less satisfaction to their provokers than the one who is very reactive and becomes easily upset.

If your child is being upset by other children, first give her some sympathy. Let her know you understand how she feels. Then try and ascertain exactly what the other children are doing and saying and how your child responds. Chat to your child about how she has to learn to be a bit clever and use psychology to throw the teasers off the track. Explain that if she behaves in a different way she can encourage the teasers to give up.

Basically teasers are looking for a reaction. They want to see their victim upset, agitated, or losing their temper. Teasing becomes unsatisfactory if the teaser gets an assertive response or gets no response at all.

An assertive response

If your child is regularly teased by a particular child then try and work out the teaser's Achilles heel. What retaliatory names can your child think of that might deter the teaser from carrying on?

No response

If you suspect your child over-reacts then use role-play to demonstrate for her what is happening. Let her play the part of the teaser while you give an exaggerated performance of being upset or angry. Ham this up a bit. Then ask your child to tease you again only this time you take absolutely no notice of her provocation.

Ask her which of your responses encouraged her to carry on teasing. This will help her understand for herself that over-reacting encourages the baiting and teasing and ensures it continues.

Change roles and give your child an opportunity to practice being indifferent while you make teasing comments. Praise her for her non-response. This will give your child confidence in her ability to cope better next time.

Warn her it might take a little while for the teasers to tire of trying, so it's important she can hold out with her non-response. If neither tactic works – the assertive response or the non-response – and the teasing seems cruel and relentless, then you may be dealing with psychological bullying and should take the same steps as you would with any other case of bullying.

If your child is bullied

Recent research suggests bullying is a more common problem than we might think. One child in five is bullied occasionally according to one study while some other research finds over a third of children are bullied badly enough to describe the experience as 'terrifying'.

Bullying may involve verbal abuse and cruel jibes, physical attacks and beatings, or it may involve threats – sometimes with extortion, perhaps with the victim expected to hand over pocket money or lunch money or to carry out some humiliating act. Sometimes the victim's personal possessions are attacked – clothes and kit thrown around or damaged. The common factor of all bullying is that one child or group of children use their power to hurt a weaker victim.

Who is bullied?
As with name-calling and teasing, the victim often tends to be a child who is 'different' – smaller, fatter, weaker or with some disability. However, the high proportion of children who are bullied at some time clearly indicates many children who don't have such difficulties can find themselves victims of bullying.

How can you recognise bullying?
Children may find it very difficult to admit they are being bullied. They may be afraid to tell, especially if the bullies have threatened them. In addition, children often feel humiliated and ashamed when they are bullied. They feel there must be something wrong with them. You may therefore not know straight away if your child is suffering although the chances are you will become aware that there is something the matter.

A child who is being bullied may:

- become quiet, tearful or withdrawn;
- be reluctant to go to school and may try and take time off;
- come home with bruises which don't have a convincing explanation;
- have possessions which get mysteriously damaged or go missing;
- come home late or by a different route.

How to help your child
Encourage your child to talk to you and to explain precisely what is happening. Show you sympathise. Give moral support and try and help your child realise bullying does not reflect badly on her but only on the bullies. If the situation is not too serious and your child wants to try and handle it alone discuss some of the following tactics.

- Find a friend or friends and stick with them.

- Don't skulk around on your own in lonely places.

- If the bullies are calling names then laugh or walk away.

- Think up an insulting name for the bully preferably one which highlights one of his/her weaknesses or peculiarities. Your child may or may not choose to use this name but it helps to cut the bully down to size in your child's imagination.

If the bullying is happening on the way to or from school perhaps you or an elder sibling can accompany the child on their journey.

Parents are often in a dilemma about whether or not to advise their children to stand their ground and fight or to run away. The chances are a child who is picked on does not feel strong enough to fight back. Let your child know it's alright to run away if they are attacked.

One of the most destructive things about bullying is that it undermines a child's self-confidence. Apart from the physical dangers this is one reason why it should never be allowed to go on for any length of time. Try and compensate by building up a child's confidence – show you appreciate her and encourage your child to follow hobbies and activities which will help improve her self-image.

Further steps

If the child is in physical danger or the bullying goes on for more than a few days you should inform the school. Many schools take a very strong stand against bullying and make it clear they will not allow this behaviour – even to the point of suspending offenders for several days or longer. Our children have no choice about attending school and it is only right that we should do everything possible to protect them while they are there.

If your child's school does not take strong enough action to stamp out bullying then you should contact the Chair of the Governors or speak to your parent governors. Governors would not want their school to get a reputation for tolerating bullies.

Is your child a bully?

Bullies have parents too and it can be as great a shock to discover your child is bullying as being bullied. Like their victims, bullies are children with problems. They often have low self-esteem and feel powerless in some aspects of their lives and take their feelings of inadequacy out on other children. For example, the child who feels hopeless at academic subjects or who is bossed around by parents or an elder sibling builds herself up by literally throwing her weight around with children who are less strong and assertive than herself. Confident, happy, well-balanced children don't need to bully others.

If you discover your child is bullying, you must first make it clear you will not allow such behaviour. Help her to understand how much pain they inflict on their victim.

Then look at your child's life. What are the stresses and strains in her life? Do arguments tend to be settled by physical force at home? Does your child feel put down either at home or at school? Is she short of friends? Does she need more positive attention and encouragement? Build up your child's self-confidence and help her to feel good about herself.

Some useful addresses

Advisory Centre for Education (ACE),
18 Victoria Park Square,
London E2 9PE.

British Dyslexia Association,
98 London Road,
Reading,
0734 668271/2.

The Department of Education and Science,
Elizabeth House,
York Road,
London SE1 7PH.

The Dyslexia Institute,
133 Gresham Road,
Staines TW18 2AJ.

Education Otherwise,
25 Common Lane,
Hemingford Abbots,
Cambridgeshire CE18 9AN.

Independent Schools Information Service (ISIS),
56 Buckingham Gate,
London SW1E 6AH.

KIDSCAPE,
The World Trade Centre,
3rd Floor,
Europe House,
London E1 9AA.

National Association for Gifted Children,
South Audley Street,
London W1Y 5DQ.

National Confederation of Parent Teacher Associations,
2 Ebbsfleet Industrial Estate,
Stonebridge Road,
Northfleet,
Gravesend,
Kent.